9/1/9
~~24.95~~

ANNUS MIRABILIS

MORE LATIN FOR EVERYDAY LIFE

ANNUS MIRABILIS

MORE LATIN FOR EVERYDAY LIFE

Mark Walker

Mellitae Meae:
semper mihi dulcior quam Mel

First published 2009

The History Press
The Mill, Brimscombe Port
Stroud, Gloucestershire, GL5 2QG
www.thehistorypress.co.uk

British Library Cataloguing in Publication Data.
A catalogue record for this book is available from the British Library.

ISBN 978 0 7524 4832 9

Typesetting and origination by The History Press
Printed in Great Britain

CONTENTS

INTRODUCTION

More Latin for Everyday Life – yes, but not just more of the same. In *Annus Horribilis* we began our Latin studies with examples drawn from everyday life; in *Annus Mirabilis* we will become more ambitious, exploring new topics and extending the original quotidian concept to encompass those many different kinds of Latin – from ephemeral notes to letters to literary works – that have been written and used 'every day' from antiquity almost to the present day.

In the first book, some Roman inscriptions notwithstanding, we encountered a great deal of Latin from the medieval period. But the Church and the medieval world were not, to coin a phrase, the Alpha and Omega of post-Roman Latin. From antiquity right up to the end of the eighteenth century – a period of some two thousand years – Latin remained central to all aspects of Western culture. The modern dominance of vernacular languages and the sidelining of the Classics curriculum in recent times has tended to obscure this important point. Even in modern university Classics departments you will find people whose interest in Latin is restricted to the works of about a dozen or so canonical authors, all of whom lived in the two centuries around the beginning of our era. Such a narrow focus seems almost intentionally perverse in the face of so many centuries of important, stimulating and often beautiful Latin literature. Can any Latinist really fail to be moved by the power of the *Dies Irae* or the pathos of the *Stabat Mater*? (*Annus Horribilis*, Chapters 11 and 12.) Can any Latinist really think that Thomas More's *Utopia* or Peter Martyr's vivid account of Columbus' voyages are *infra dignitatem* merely because the writers did not wield Latin as their native language? Are Erasmus' letters any less fascinating, revealing and funny than Pliny's? And is there anything from antiquity to match the impassioned exchanges in the correspondence of Heloise and Abelard?

Annus Mirabilis, then, casts its net a little wider than that of its predecessor, taking in a little of what is now called Renaissance Latin or Neo-Latin, a woefully underappreciated corpus. Hopefully after reading (and enjoying!) these selections, you the reader will be inspired to be more adventurous in your own ramblings through the glories of Latin literature.

You will also find here many other examples of 'everyday' Latin. There are enough and more than enough learned tomes about Classical Latin literature to make me very wary of encroaching on their hallowed territory, but — *carpe diem*! — in our pursuit of the 'everyday' language it would be remiss to neglect entirely the letters of Cicero and some of his Roman successors (Chapter 4) who were, after all, the inspiration for all who followed. We will also explore more humble Roman correspondence from the families of soldiers stationed on Hadrian's wall and civilians visiting the spa town of *Aquae Sulis* (Chapter 1). The tradition of epistolary Latin based on the Ciceronian model survived through the Middle Ages, as the letters of Heloise and Abelard reveal, and it positively blossomed thereafter (Chapter 5). We shall also see that Latin was the language in which many of the most important scientific and philosophical ideas of the modern age were expressed (Chapter 6). And let us not forget the fascinating and seductive topic of Latin poetry — arguably the greatest literary achievement of the ancient Romans — which never ceased to flourish in every age, from graceful medieval lyrics (Chapter 2) and elegant epitaphs (Chapter 3), to solemn and satirical imitations of Classical models (Chapter 7).

Taken together the two books, *Annus Horribilis* and *Annus Mirabilis*, can be viewed as an attempt to answer that irritating question every Latin student has to endure over and over again from bemused interlocutors: 'Why learn Latin?' — Because it is so much more than just the dead language of a fallen empire.

How to use this book

Many of the texts featured here are more challenging than those in *Annus Horribilis*. Lest you quail at the prospect, gentle reader, be reassured that I have provided plentiful notes for each selection. Readers of *Annus Horribilis* will be familiar with the format and well equipped to tackle everything here. Other readers will nonetheless be able to enjoy *Annus Mirabilis* as an independent book in its own right — a basic grounding in Latin grammar and a good dictionary at your elbow are all the prerequisites you will need. My own pedantically literal renderings are to be found at the end, so you can always peek at the English version if you get stuck.

It is my hope that the sheer diversity of material presented here will make *Annus Mirabilis* more than just a rewarding follow-up to its predecessor; it should also make a suitable companion to any other Latin course, since the inherent interest and comparative rarity of many of the selections will complement more traditional approaches, giving students who have thus far only encountered the Classical authors an opportunity to delve into new areas equally enjoyable.

Hoc donum dono tibi tam parvum lepidumque:
Accipe tam laete quam lepideque dedi.

Mark Walker

CHAPTER 1

CURSES, COINS AND INVITATIONS

In this opening chapter we catch a glimpse of the everyday life and language of ordinary ancient Romans. It is easy to forget that the literary Latin of the Classical period is almost exclusively the work of an educated elite: the speeches of Cicero or the poems of Virgil are distinctly highbrow specimens of written Latin, which in general was far more often preoccupied with mundane activities just as written English is today – shopping lists and To-Do lists, short letters to friends (the ancient Roman equivalent of emails), birthday invitations and hurriedly scribbled notes. Examples of such *ephemera* have been recovered in various locations across the Roman Empire, notably in Britain at Vindolanda on Hadrian's Wall. By dint of their very ordinariness these texts bring us closer to the people who wrote them: not literary giants, philosophers or poets, but people like us.

CURSES

The curse-tablets or *defixiones* found in the Roman bath complex at *Aquae Sulis* in Bath, Somerset, and at other sacred sites are personal messages usually inscribed on small lead sheets, addressed to a god or goddess in a spirit of unabashed anger against those who have wronged the writer. The texts reveal much information about the religious and magical-superstitious beliefs held in the ancient world, as well as the unvarying bent of human nature. Though most of us don't curse people anymore (publicly at any rate), we can all sympathise with the impulse that prompted such heartfelt outpourings.

Defixiones

The word *defixiones* is derived from the verb *defigo*, *defigere* 'fasten down', reflecting both the physical and metaphorical nature of the tablets – they were pierced with an actual nail, perhaps for the same reason that people stick pins in Voodoo dolls, since the writer wanted the object of his or her anger to be 'held' or 'fixed' by the curse.

The texts as restored by scholars (see recommended reading below) provide fascinating examples of the difficulties of translation and interpretation even after the words themselves have been painstakingly deciphered. I have not attempted to copy the layout as it appears in scholarly publications, nor have I indicated the many gaps or uncertain readings – our concern here is solely to enjoy making translations, thereby bringing these voices from the past back to life.

1. *From the Temple of Nodens in Uley, Gloucestershire*

Devo Nodenti Silvianus anilum perdedit demediam partem donavit Nodenti inter quibus nomen Seniciani nollis petmittas sanitatem donec perferat usque templum Nodentis.

Notes:

1. Devo Nodenti – dative of the addressee; Nodens was the Celtic god of healing; *Devo* for *Divo*, dative of *Divus*, 'divine'
2. Silvianus – the writer: he has lost (*perdedit*, perfect tense of *perdo*, more usually spelt *perdidit*) a ring (*anilum*, usually spelt *anulum*)
3. demediam partem donavit – he has given (*donavit*) to Nodens (*Nodenti*, dative again) one half of its value; *demediam* is more usually *dimidiam*, feminine accusative of adjective *dimidius*, agreeing with *partem*
4. inter quibus nomen Seniciani – sc. *illos* after *inter*: 'among those (people)', and *est* with *quibus* = dative of possession (q.v. *mihi nomen est* from *Annus Horribilis*, Ch. 2): 'to those whom there is the name (of)' so 'among those who have the name of Senicianus' – the man whom Silvianus suspects of stealing his ring
5. nollis petmittas – subjunctives (regularly spelt *nolis permittas*), bad Latin for *noli permittere*: 'do not permit good health (*sanitatem*)'
6. perferat – present subjunctive (spelt correctly!), 'until he shall deliver (the ring)'
7. usque templum Nodentis – 'right up to the Temple of Nodens'
8. some time later, the word *Rediviva*, 'renewed', was added to the inscription, indicating that Senicianus was still apparently

both unrepentant and healthy, and that Silvianus was still waiting for his ring!

The following four selections are all *defixiones* from *Aquae Sulis* in Bath:

2. *Vilbia*

qui mihi VILBIAM involavit sic liquat comodo aqua ... qui eam involavit ...
Velvinna Exsupereus Verianus Severinus Augustalis Comitianus Minianus
Catus Germanilla Iovina.

Notes:

1. Discovered in 1880, this was the first of the Bath curses to be unearthed
2. *VILBIAM* – it is not known what *VILBIA* was; one tentative suggestion is that the word should be *fibulam*, 'a brooch'
3. involavit – perfect tense of *involo*, 'seize', 'steal'
4. liquat – subjunctive, possibly for *liqueat*, 'may he become liquid'
5. comodo – for *quomodo*, 'in the same manner', take with *sic*: 'as liquid as water (*aqua*)'
6. qui eam involavit – '(s)he who has stolen it (i.e. *Vlbia*)', after which there is a gap then a list of names
7. Velvinna ... Jovina – the list is a mixture of Roman and Celtic names, presumably all those suspected of the theft.

3. *A stolen cloak*

Minervae deae Suli donavi furem qui caracallam meam involavit si servus si
liber si baro si mulier hoc donum non redemat nessi sanguine suo.

Notes:

1. Minervae deae Suli – dative after *donavi*: he dedicates the thief (accusative *furem*) to the goddess; the Romans identified the native Celtic deity Sulis with their Minerva
2. caracallam – a hooded cloak of Celtic design made fashionable by the Emperor Caracalla (reigned A.D. 211–217) who derived his nickname from it; his notoriety was appropriate for someone

who sported a 'hoodie'
3.   involavit – see *VILBIA* above
4.   si baro si mulier – equivalent of *si vir si femina*; in Classical Latin a *baro* is a 'blockhead' or 'lout'
5.   redemat – for *redimat*, subjunctive of *redimo* (English: 'redeem'): 'let him not purchase this gift (*hoc donum*) …'
6.   nessi – for *nisi*: '… unless with his own blood'.

4. *An oath*

Uricalus Docilosa uxor sua Docilis filius suus et Docilina Decentinus frater suus Alogiosa nomina eorum qui iuraverunt ad fontem deae Sulis pridie idus Apriles quicumque illic periuraverit deae Suli facias illum sanguine suo illud satisfacere.

Notes:
1.   The text begins with a list of people connected with Uricalus: his wife Docilosa, his son Docilis, Docilina (his daughter?), his brother Decentinus and someone else called Alogiosa
2.   nomina eorum qui iuraverunt – the list of names explained, they are the 'names of those (*eorum*) who swore an oath (*iuraverunt*)'
3.   ad fontem – at the sacred spring of the goddess Sulis
4.   pridie idus Apriles – 'the day before the Ides of April', i.e. the 12th – see *Annus Horribilis*, Ch. 5 for Roman dates
5.   quicumque – 'whosoever'; the *-cumque* ending of pronouns = '-ever'; *illic* – 'there', 'in that place'
6.   periuraverit – perfect subjunctive of *periuro* (also spelt *peiero*), the opposite of *iurare*: English 'perjure'
7.   facias … satisfacere – literally, 'may you make him to make amends', so 'see to it that he makes amends …'; *facias* is present subjunctive; the verb *satisfacio* takes the dative, in the sense of 'give satisfaction to …', here to the goddess 'with his own blood (*sanguine suo*)'.

5. *A bloody curse*

Basilia donat in templum Martis anilum argenteum si servus si liber medius fuerit vel aliquid de hoc noverit ut sanguine et liminibus et omnibus membris configatur vel etiam intestinis excomesis omnibus habe(at) is qui anilum involavit vel qui medius fuerit.

Notes:

1. Basilia – she is donating a silver ring (*anilum* = *anulum*) to the Temple of Mars
2. medius fuerit – probably this means 'has been a witness (of the crime)', with the sense of *medius* as the person in the midst of things, however unwittingly; the phrase *medius fidius* means 'I call heaven to witness'
3. vel aliquid de hoc noverit – 'or knows something (*aliquid*) about this'
4. ut … configatur – *ut* + passive subjunctive (see Appendix) of *configo*, here meaning 'let him be struck down' or 'cursed'
5. sanguine et liminibus et omnibus membris – ablatives, '(in respect of) blood and eyes (= *luminibus*) and all his limbs'
6. intestinis excomesis omnibus – ablative absolute (see Appendix), 'with all his intestines having been eaten away'
7. habe(at) – either an imperative or subjunctive, the sense is unclear, but it could mean, 'let him be done for', a term used of gladiators receiving a fatal wound.

COINS

Latin doesn't get more commonplace than the highly abbreviated *sententiae* found on Roman coins, a practice that continues to the present day (see *Annus Horribilis*, Chapter 4) which if nothing else reminds us that Latin really is our common currency. These numismatic texts, naturally, weren't written by our putative *vir* on the Aventine *Omnibus*, but such little Latin phrases must have been a solid reminder to everyone in the Roman Empire of their shared language and culture.

Fortunately, Roman coins survive in great numbers, especially from the Imperial period when minting currency was a quick and easy way for an emperor or aspiring ruler to publicise his identity and establish his authority. Generally coin inscriptions consist of nothing more than the emperor's titles on the obverse (front) side written clockwise around a portrait. On the reverse side the titles might

Coin Denominations

Under Augustus, the coinage consisted of the following types:

Aureus
Denarius
Sestertius
Dupondius
As
Quadrans

1 *Aureus* = 25 *Denarii*
1 *Denarius* = 4 *Sestertii* = 8 *Dupondii* = 16 *Asses* = 64 *Quadrans*

Later Imperial coins include the *Antoninianus* and the gold *Solidus*

continue, or there could be a single-word dedication to a helpful god or goddess such as *Victoria* or *Concordia*, or simply the initials S C, *Senatus Consulto*, 'by a decree of the Senate' – the latter demonstrating that the emperor's coinage is from a legitimate source.

Just two examples of imperial coins from different eras:

1. *As of Claudius (A.D. 41-54)*

The obverse depicts a bust of Claudius with the legend around the perimeter:

TI CLAVDIVS CAESAR AVG P M TR P IMP

The reverse has a portrait of the goddess Minerva, underneath which is simply:

S C

Expanded:

Tiberius Claudius Caesar Augustus Pontifex Maximus Tribunicia Potestate Imperator Senatus Consulto.

Notes:

1. Claudius was born Tiberius Claudius Drusus, afterwards adding Nero Germanicus to his name. He was only a very minor member of the imperial family, grandson of Livia by her first marriage, who then married Augustus, and nephew of the Tiberius who became emperor after Augustus

2. Tribunicia Potestate − '(invested) with the power of a tribune'; Augustus assumed for himself the power but not the actual office of tribune (an old Republican bulwark for the common people against the aristocracy) in order to demonstrate his concern for the common folk; later emperors adopted the same purely honorary title, but it did not necessarily imply they had any special concern for the masses

3. Senatus − genitive of the fourth declension noun *Senatus*. *Consulto* − ablative of *consultum*, the neuter form of the perfect participle passive of the verb *consulo, consulere*, 'consult'.

2. Antoninianus of Gordian III (A.D. 238-244)

The obverse has a bust of Gordian wearing a radiate crown and the words:

> IMP GORDIANUS PIVS FEL AVG

The reverse depicts the goddess Roma seated holding a sceptre and small winged victory on a globe:

> ROMAE AETERNAE

Expanded:

Imperator Gordianus Pius Felix Augustus Romae Aeternae.

Notes:

1. Gordian III was proclaimed emperor while still a boy in A.D. 238 (aged 13), the year in which both his father and grandfather had held supreme power for less than two months and their successors, Balbinus and Pupienus, had lasted only

a little longer. He defeated the Persians in 242, but was then assassinated by his praetorian prefect and successor Philip (244-249)

2. Augustus – by this period the title *Augustus* was reserved for the emperor, while *Caesar* denoted his junior colleague(s)

3. pius felix – these had become traditional epithets; *pius* was first accorded to Antoninus Pius (A.D. 138-161) and then adopted by his successors; Gordian may have been *pius* but he does not seem to have been *felix*

4. *Romae Aeternae* – dative, since the coin is dedicated to the goddess Roma.

THE VINDOLANDA LETTERS

In Chapter 14 of *Annus Horribilis* we encountered some typical Roman inscriptions from buildings, altars and other monuments. But not all Roman inscriptions were carved in stone: the Roman fort of Vindolanda on Hadrian's Wall has yielded hundreds of small wooden 'notebooks', fragile slivers of wood which have remarkably survived 2000 years. Most are fragmentary but many have been painstakingly deciphered to produce a vivid picture of daily life on the Roman frontier *c*.A.D. 100: requests for leave, reports on troop numbers and enemy activity, accounts and receipts, endless lists of goods in store and required, as well as many personal letters to friends and family.

1. *A birthday invitation*

Claudia Severa Lepidinae suae salutem, III Idus Septembres soror ad diem sollemnem natalem meum rogo libenter facias ut venias ad nos iucundiorem mihi diem interventu tuo factura … sperabo te soror vale soror anima mea ita valeam karissima et have. Sulpiciae Lepidinae Cerialis a Severa.

Vindolanda online

A searchable database of the Vindolanda tablets can be found at
http://vindolanda.csad.ox.ac.uk/index.shtml

Notes:

1. This and the following example can be found in Bowman's *Life and Letters on the Roman Frontier* (see recommended reading below); as with the *defixiones* I have made no attempt to reproduce the actual layout of the texts or indicate the many gaps, abbreviations or uncertain readings

2. Lepidinae suae – dative of the addressee after *salutem*, the traditional opening of a letter, 'greetings to …'; translate *suae* ('her own') as 'dear'

3. III Idus Septembres – 'the third day before the Ides', i.e. the 11th – see *Annus Horribilis*, Ch. 5

4. soror – vocative, Lepidina is Claudia's sister

5. ad diem … natalem – 'my birthday'; a *sollemnis* is a celebration, here 'my birthday party'; *rogo* – 'I ask, invite'

6. libenter – adverb, 'with pleasure', 'gladly'; take this either with *rogo* ('I invite you with pleasure') or with subjunctive *facias*

7. facias ut venias – 'be sure that you come to us (*ad nos*)'; *facias* is here a mild form of command, followed by an *ut* + subjunctive clause (see Appendix)

8. factura – future participle (see Appendix) to express purpose: '(in order) to make'; *iucundiorem … diem* – comparative adjective, 'the day more enjoyable'; *interventu tuo* – ablative, 'by your arrival'

9. … – there are several gaps and fragments after *factura*

10. sperabo – future tense, 'I will expect you (i.e. look forward to your arrival)'

11. anima mea – a term of endearment, 'my (dear) soul' = 'my darling'

12. ita valeam – subjunctive of *valeo*, common at the end of a letter: 'so I take my leave' or just 'goodbye'

13. karissima et have – for *carissima*, 'my dearest', and *ave* – q.v. Catullus: *ave atque vale*, 'hail and farewell'

14. Sulpiciae … a Severa – the address on the back of the note: 'to Sulpicia Lepidina (wife) of Cerialis from Severa' – the ommission of the word for wife is common.

2. *Greetings from an old messmate*

Chrauttius Veldeio suo fratri contubernali antiquo plurimam salutem et rogo te Veldei frater miror quod mihi tot tempus nihil rescripsti a parentibus nostris si quid audieris … in quo numero sit et illum a me salutabis verbis meis et Virilem veterinarium rogabis illum ut forficem quam mihi promissit pretio mittas per aliquem de nostris … opto sis felicissimus, vale. Londini Veldedeio equisioni cos. a Chrauttio fratre.

Notes:

1. Veldeio suo fratri contubernali antiquo – dative of the addressee, the brother and messmate (*contubernalis*) of Chrauttius
2. plurimam salutem – 'many greetings'
3. Veldei frater – vocative
4. miror quod – 'I am surprised that …'
5. tot tempus – 'for such a long time'; *tot* is indeclinable
6. si quid audieris – perfect subjunctive (because an indirect question), properly spelt *audiveris*: 'if you have heard anything'
7. in quo numero sit – there is a gap before this phrase; *numerus* here is in the military sense of 'a unit'
8. salutabis – future tense, 'you will greet him (*illum*) from me (*a me*) in my own words (*verbis meis*)'
9. rogabis – another future tense
10. veterinarium – Virilis is the military vet
11. ut … mittas – *ut* + subjunctive (see Appendix): Chrauttius wants Veldeius to ask Virilis if he (Veldeius) can send the scissors or shears (*forficem*, nominative *forfex*) which Virilis has promised to Chrauttius
12. pretio – ablative, 'for a price' – Chrauttius has already agreed to pay Virilis for the shears (*quam mihi promissit*)
13. per aliquem de nostris – 'via someone of our friends'
14. opto sis felicissimus – 'I pray you may be very fortunate'
15. Londini – the address at the back of the note: *Londini* is locative, 'at London'; *Veldeideio* – dative, note the variant spelling; an *equiso* is a groom or stable-boy; *cos.* short for *consularis*, 'a man of consular rank,', i.e. the provincial governor (*propraetor*), so 'to the governor's groom'.

Recommended Reading:

A. K. Bowman   *Life and Letters on the Roman Frontier*
                    British Museum Press

An accessible volume giving the background to the Vindolanda writing
tablets and examples thereof.

B. Cunliffe (ed.)   The Temple of Sulis Minerva at Bath Vol. II:
                    The Finds from the Sacred Spring
                    Oxford University Committee for Archaeology
                    Monograph 16

A scholarly work containing the full texts of many of the *defixiones*

CHAPTER 2

LYRICAL LATIN

Much of what is beautiful in Latin is verse. The conciseness of expression and flexibility of word order offered by the Latin language make it peculiarly well suited to being cast into poetic form. So in this and the next chapter we will explore Latin poetry. Then, in the final chapter, we will return to the subject of verse with a more sympathetic appreciation of such arcane matters as metre and accent.

In *Annus Horribilis* we encountered some outstanding examples of medieval Latin verse, notably the *Dies Irae*, the *Stabat Mater* and the *O Fortuna* from the *Carmina Burana* collection. These differ from the Classical poetry of Roman authors like Virgil, Ovid and Catullus in three important respects:

1. Such medieval verse was generally intended to be sung, whereas Classical Latin verse was for recitation (the exception that proves the rule being the *Carmina* of Horace, which may have been written with musical accompaniment in mind)

2. Medieval verse is generally accentual, i.e. it is poetry whose metrical rhythm or beat is based on the stress-accents of the words, just as is the case with English poetry

3. Medieval examples often feature rhymed line-endings, again in contrast to Classical verse. Rhyme signals the end of each line and creates an especially pleasing effect when sung.

Although Classical quantitative verse continued to be written throughout the Middle Ages, it is this stress-accented, rhyming lyric that is the distinctive creation of the medieval period, and the form in which its greatest works were written. In Chapter 3 we will explore the other kind of Latin poetry, quantitative verse. But for now, a short explanation of some common types of accentual verse.

IAMBIC RHYTHM

Consider the following lines:

> Attend all ye who list to hear our noble England's praise;
> I tell of the thrice famous deeds she wrought in ancient days
> When that great fleet invincible against her bore in vain
> The richest spoils of Mexico, the stoutest hearts of Spain.
>
> (Macaulay, *Armada*)

The lilt or rhythm of these lines is caused by regular alternation of accented and unaccented syllables, in this pattern:

```
   /         /       /     /         /     /           /
At-tend all ye who list to hear our no-ble Eng-land's praise
```
i.e. 'di-dum, di-dum, di-dum' etc.

Each 'di-dum' is known as a 'foot'. Any given verse line consists of several such 'feet' arranged in a particular order. The ordering of the feet determines the metre of the verse.

In this case the foot is the same throughout: an iamb – so this metre is called iambic. The natural stress accents of English words makes them peculiarly well suited to such iambic patterns. For example:

> If music be the food of love, play on
>
> (Shakespeare, *Twelfth Night*)

This is the classic iambic pentameter of English blank verse. *Iambic* because each foot is a 'di-dum' *iamb*, and *pentameter* because each line consists of a chain of five *iambs*:

```
  1        2       3         4        5
   /        /         /        /         /
If mu- ¦ -sic be ¦ the food ¦ of love ¦ play on
```

The iambic rhythm is less common in Latin than English, but there are some famous medieval hymns which use it.

TWO IAMBIC HYMNS

1. O Quanta Qualia

This hymn by Peter Abelard (1079–1142) employs an iambic rhythm in lines of 12 syllables (or half-lines of six syllables each if you prefer). We will hear more about Abelard in Chapter 5, but for now it is sufficient to observe that not only was he a brilliant scholar, he was also a celebrated composer whose love songs were once the toast of Paris. In his later monastic life he composed a complete hymnal for the Monastery of the Paraclete where his beloved Heloise was abbess. Sadly all his secular songs are lost, and only a handful of his sacred works have been positively identified in manuscript sources, the best known being *O Quanta Qualia*.

> *O quanta qualia sunt illa sabbata*
> *quae semper celebrat superna curia,*
> *quae fessis requies, quae merces fortibus,*
> *cum erit omnia Deus in omnibus.*
>
> *Vera Ierusalem est illa civitas,*
> *cuius pax iugis est, summa iucunditas,*
> *ubi non praevenit rem desiderium,*
> *nec desiderio minus est praemium.*
>
> *Quis rex, quae curia, quale palatium,*
> *quae pax, quae requies, quod illud gaudium,*
> *huius participes exponant gloriae,*
> *si quantum sentiunt, possint exprimere.*
>
> *Nostrum est interim mentem erigere*
> *et totis patriam votis appetere,*
> *et ad Ierusalem a Babylonia*
> *post longa regredi tandem exsilia.*

Illic molestiis finitis omnibus
securi cantica Sion cantibimus,
et iuges gratias de donis gratiae
beata referet plebs tibi, Domine.

Illic ex sabbato succedet sabbatum,
perpes laetitia sabbatizantium,
nec ineffabiles cessabunt iubili,
quos decantabimus et nos et angeli.

Perenni Domino perpes sit gloria,
ex quo sunt, per quem sunt, in quo sunt omnia;
ex quo sunt, Pater est, per quem sunt, Filius,
in quo sunt, Patris et Filii Spiritus.

Notes:

1. *quanta qualia* – *quanta* and *qualia* (from *qualis*) are both neuter plural agreeing with the noun *sabbata*. The translation depends on whether we punctuate *O quanta, qualia sunt* or *O quanta qualia* – the first option yields 'O how many, of what sort are the Sabbaths', the second 'O how many kinds are the Sabbaths'. Its tempting to add 'and' in English: 'how many *and* of what kind'. Helen Waddell in *Medieval Latin Lyrics* paraphrases beautifully: 'How mighty are the Sabbaths, how mighty and how deep'

2. *sabbata* – plural of neuter noun *sabbatum*, a word unsurprisingly derived from Hebrew

3. *superna curia* – the *Curia* was the building in which the Roman Senate assembled, so metonymy for any council or governing body, here a celestial one

4. *fessis ... fortibus* – datives, 'for the weary ... the strong'

5. *omnia Deus in omnibus* – literally: 'God will be (*erit*) all things in everything'

6. *iugis* – 'constant, continual' i.e. '(Jerusalem's) peace is everlasting'

7. *ubi non praevenit rem desiderium* – 'when desire (*desiderium*) does not come before (*praevenit*) the matter itself (*rem*)', i.e. desire does not anticipate its fulfilment; *nec desiderio minus est praemium* – 'the reward (*praemium*) is not less (*minus*) than the desire (ablative *desiderio*)', i.e. anything desired is instantly granted

8. exponant – subjunctive: 'let them expound what king, what council, what sort of palace (*palatium*) …'; who is expounding? The *participes huius gloriae*, 'the participants of this glory'

9. si … exprimere – 'if they are able (subjunctive plural of *possum*) to express (*exprimere*) how much (*quantum*) they feel (*sentiunt*)'

10. nostrum est … erigere – 'it is for us (*nostrum*, literally 'ours') to raise up (*erigere*) our hearts (*mentem*)'

11. totis … appetere – 'to seek (*appetere*) our native land (*patriam*) with all our prayers (*totis votis*)

12. ad Ierusalem – Classical Latin would not normally include the preposition *ad* to express motion towards a city; here perhaps to make the distinction clear: from Bablyon *to* Jerusalem

13. post longa … exsilia – 'after a long exile', for which see the Book of *Exodus* and Psalm 136 in the Vulgate, *Super flumina Babylonis*, 'By the rivers of Babylon' (Psalm 137 in the King James version)

14. regredi – active infinitive of deponent *regredior*: 'to return'

15. illic molestiis finitis omnibus – 'in that place (*illic*) after all our troubles (*omnibus molestiis*) have been ended': ablative absolute (see Appendix) with perfect participle passive of *finio*, 'put to an end'

16. securi cantica Sion cantibimus – adjective *securus*, 'free from fear, untroubled', nominative plural; *cantibimus* – future tense: 'we will sing'; *cantica* – neuter plural accusative; *Sion* – indeclinable, 'of Sion'

17. iuges gratias – we have already seen *pax iugis*, here plural 'everlasting thanks'

18. de donis gratiae – 'for the gifts (*de donis*) of grace (*gratiae*)'; note wordplay with preceding *gratias* ('thanks')

19. beata … plebs – 'the blessed multitude'; *referet* – future tense, 'will give back'

20. succedet – another future tense, 'will come after, succeed (to)' followed by the dative in Classical Latin, but here ablative e*x sabbato*, 'Sabbath follows Sabbath'

21. perpes laetitia sabbatizantium – 'the continual happiness of those who are celebrating the Sabbaths'; *sabbatizantium* is genitive plural of the present participle of the Church Latin verb *sabbatizare*, 'to observe the Sabbath'

22. cessabunt – still in the future tense, 'will cease'; *ineffabiles iubili* – 'unutterable cries (English 'ineffable') *iubilus* is a late-Latin coinage

23. quos ... angeli – 'which (i.e. the cries of joy) both (*et ... et*) we and the angels will chant (future of *decantare*)'

24. sit – subjunctive (q.v. *fiat lux!*) of *est* with dative of possession *Perenni Domino* = 'let eternal God have perpetual glory'

25. ex quo ... per quem ... in quo – 'from whom ... through whom ... in whom'; *sunt omnia* – 'there are all things'

26. Pater est ... Filius ... Spiritus – 'he is the Father from whom ... the Son through whom ... the Spirit in whom'; understand *omnia* again: 'there are all things'.

2. *Veni Creator Spiritus*

This iambic hymn for Pentecost is attributed to Rabanus (or Hrabanus) Maurus (*c*.780–856), a pupil of Alcuin of York. It has proved popular with composers – Mahler included a version of it as the opening of his Eighth Symphony (1907) – and it continues to be set: in 1997, composer Carl Rütti published a 40-part version for unaccompanied choir (see recommended listening below).

> *Veni Creator Spiritus,*
> *mentes tuorum visita,*
> *imple superna gratia,*
> *quae tu creasti pectora*

> *Qui Paraclitus diceris,*
> *altissimi donum Dei,*
> *fons vivus, ignis, caritas,*
> *et spiritalis unctio.*

> *Tu septiformis munere,*
> *dextrae Dei tu digitus,*

The Carolingian Renaissance

Alcuin of York (*c*.735–804) was a leading light of the so-called Carolingian Renaissance, a flowering of learning fostered by the Emperor Charlemagne (*c*.742–814), during which Latin began to be taught systematically in order to ensure that priests could properly read and disseminate the text of the Vulgate Bible. Alcuin's pupil Rabanus Maurus, later Archbishop of Mainz, wrote works on grammar as well as producing an encyclopaedia.

tu rite promisso Patris,
sermone ditans guttura.

Accende lumen sensibus,
infunde amorem cordibus,
infirma nostri corporis
virtute firmans perpeti.

Hostem repellas longius,
pacemque dones protinus,
ductore sic te praevio,
vitemus omne noxium.

Per te sciamus da Patrem,
noscamus atque Filium,
teque utriusque Spiritum
credamus omni tempore.

Deo Patri sit gloria
et Filio qui a mortuis
surrexit ac Paraclito
in saeculorum saecula.

Notes:

1. *veni* – imperative, 'come'; *Spiritus* is fourth declension, so vocative ending *–us* (not *–e* as second declension, e.g. *Domine*); take *Creator Spiritus* either as adjective-noun 'Creator Spirit' or as two distinct nouns, 'Creator, Holy Spirit'

2. visita … imple – more imperatives, 'visit … fill'

3. mentes tuorum – 'the souls of yours' i.e. 'of your own people'; *mens* here = 'soul'

4. pectora – after *imple*: 'fill the breasts/hearts of those which you have created'; *superna gratia* – ablative, 'with celestial grace'

5. qui Paraclitus diceris – *Paraclitus* = 'the Comforter'. I have seen this line variously rendered as *Qui diceris Paraclitus*, *Qui Paraclitus dicitur* and *Qui dicitur Paraclitus*. Here the accent of *Par-ac-**lit**-us* falls on the penultimate syllable, but in the final verse (the doxology, see below) the accent falls on the antepenultimate: *Par-**ac**-lit-o*

6. spiritalis unctio – 'spiritual ointment' (English, 'unction')

7. tu septiformis munere – literally: 'you who are sevenfold
   (*septiformis*) in respect of your gift (ablative of *munus*)' i.e.
   a sevenfold gift, a reference to the seven gifts of the Lord
   outlined in *Isaiah* xi.2: wisdom, understanding, counsel,
   fortitude, knowledge, piety and fear of the Lord

8. dextrae Dei … digitus – 'the finger of God's right hand' (the
   word *manus* is understood)

9. rite – adverb, 'according to ritual' but also 'rightly, fittingly';
   promisso Patris, 'by the promise of the Father'

10. sermone ditans guttura – 'enriching (*ditans*, present participle
    of *dito*) our throats (*guttura*) with speech (ablative of *sermo*)'; a
    reference to *Acts* ii.4: 'they began to speak with other tongues
    as the Spirit gave them utterance'

11. accende … infunde – more imperatives, 'kindle a light for our
    senses (*sensibus*), pour love in our hearts (*cordibus*)'

12. firmans – present participle of *firmo*, 'fortifying the infirmities
    (*infirma*) of our body (*nostri corporis*) with perpetual virtue
    (ablative, *virtute perpeti*)'

13. repellas – present subjunctive, 'let you repel the enemy further
    (*longius*)' or simply an alternative for the imperative: 'repel the
    enemy'

14. dones – another present subjunctive, 'give'; *protinus* –
    'immediately'

15. ductore te – ablative, 'with you as our leader'; *praevio* – also
    ablative, of *praevius*, 'leading the way' (English: 'previous')

16. vitemus – another subjunctive, of *vitare*, 'to avoid'; *noxium*
    – 'harm'

17. da – imperative, 'grant (that) …'; *sciamus* … *noscamus* …
    credamus – subjunctives, 'we may know … recognise …
    believe in'; *credo* + accusative is a transitive verb = 'believe in,
    have faith in', otherwise it is intransitive and takes the dative
    when it means 'believe, trust (someone)'

18. utriusque Spiritum – 'the Spirit of both', *utrius* is genitive of
    uterque

19. Deo Patri sit gloria – dative of possession: 'let God the
    Father have glory', also datives *Filio* … *Paraclito*; this final verse is
    not part of the original hymn, but is the doxology, from the Greek
    word δοξα (*doxa*), meaning – in a Church context – 'glory'

20. mortuis surrexit – 'rose from (among) the dead', note how Latin prefers the plural where English uses a singular collective noun

21. in saeculorum saecula – the formulaic finale, literally: 'into the ages of the ages', derived from the Hebrew way of saying 'for ever and ever'.

TROCHAIC RHYTHM

If we reverse the *iamb* to make a 'dum-di' we get another type of foot known as a *trochee*, e.g.

/   /   / / /   / / /
Com-rades, leave me here a lit-tle, while as yet 'tis ear-ly morn
(Tennyson, *Locksley Hall*)

Here the stress is on the first syllable of each foot, not the second. The trochee is very commonly found in medieval Latin verse – we have already read and enjoyed these examples:

>*Dies irae, dies illa*
>*solvet saeclum in favilla,*
>*teste David cum Sibylla.*

(*Dies Irae*, see *Annus Horribilis*, Ch. 11)

and

>*Stabat Mater dolorosa,*
>*iuxta crucem lacrimosa,*
>*dum pendebat Filius*

(*Stabat Mater*, see *Annus Horribilis*, Ch. 12)

Both are in eight-syllabled trochaic metre, the stress falling on the first beat of each 'dum-di' trochee, so:

>/ /   /   /
>*Di-es ir-ae, di-es il-la*

and

>/   /   / /
>*Stab-at mat-er dol-or-o-sa*

A slightly different scheme is found in the *O Fortuna* of the *Carmina Burana*:

> *O Fortuna,*
> *velut luna*
> *statu variabilis,*
> *semper crescis*
> *aut decrescis;*
> *vita detestabilis*

(Annus Horribilis, Ch. 13)

Which is still trochaic ('dum-di') but this time each stanza consists of two four-syllable lines followed by a seven-syllable line:

```
  /       /
O For-tun-a
  /     /
vel-ut lun-a
  /     /    /    /
stat-u var-i-a-bil-is
```

TWO TROCHAIC LYRICS

1. *Ave Maris Stella*

This anonymous Vespers hymn in honour of the Virgin goes back at least as far as the ninth century, possibly earlier. The trochaic rhythm is particularly strong throughout, as most of the words consist of two syllables with the stress falling on the first syllable, e.g.

```
  /      /      /
Av-e mar-is stel-la.
```

Many composers down the centuries have found this hymn inspirational, including Byrd, Palestrina, Monteverdi, Grieg, Saint-Saëns, Elgar, Peter Maxwell Davies and, right up to the present day, Carl Rütti (who has also set the *Veni Creator Spiritus*, see above). In 2004, Cecilia McDowall composed a setting for solo soprano, chorus and string orchestra (see recommended listening below) – McDowall has also set the *Stabat Mater* and *Personent hodie*, the texts of which you'll find in *Annus Horribillis*, Chapter 12.

Ave, maris stella,   *Virgo singularis,*
Dei mater alma,   *inter omnes mitis,*
atque semper virgo,   *nos culpis solutos*
felix coeli porta.   *mites fac et castos.*

Sumens illud Ave   *Vitam praesta puram,*
Gabrielis ore,   *iter para tutum,*
funda nos in pace,   *ut videntes Jesum*
mutans Evae nomen.   *semper collaetemur.*

Solve vincla reis   *Sit laus Deo Patri,*
profer lumen caecis,   *summum Christo decus,*
mala nostra pelle,   *Spiritui Sancto,*
bona cuncta posce.   *honor, tribus unus.*

Monstra te esse matrem,
sumat per te preces
qui pro nobis natus,
tulit esse tuus.

Notes:

1. Ave – the imperative, meaning 'hail' (see *Annus Horribilis*, Ch. 2), but also here a pun on the Latin name *Eva* ('Eve')
2. maris – genitive; another pun, on the Latin name *Maria*, since the plural of neuter noun *mare* is also *maria*
3. mater alma – hence the expression *alma mater* (see *Annus Horribilis*, Ch. 3)
4. felix … porta – 'fortunate portal', the gateway through which heaven (*coeli*, genitive) entered the world
5. sumens – present participle from *sumo*, 'receiving'
6. Gabrielis ore – 'from the mouth of (the angel) Gabriel', as related in *Luke* I.28; *funda* – imperative, 'make us firm in peace'
7. mutans Evae nomen – the present participle of *muto*, 'exchanging, borrowing'; Mary borrows the name of Eve in the form of the pun *ave* but also takes on Eve's role as the

(new) mother of humanity

8. solvē ... profer ... pelle ... posce – imperatives, 'loosen (the bonds, *vincla*, neuter plural) ... bring (light) ... drive out (our evils) ... offer (all good things)'

9. reis ... caecis – datives of *reus* ('the accused') and *caecus* ('blind')

10. monstra – imperative ('show') followed by accusative + infinitive 'that ...' (see Appendix) *te matrem esse*

11. sumat – present subjunctive from *sumo*, 'let him receive'

12. tulit esse tuus – *tulit* is perfect tense of *fero*, 'bear, endure': 'allowed (himself) to be yours', i.e. Jesus who allowed himself to be born from Mary

13. singularis ... mitis – 'matchless ... gentle'

14. nos ... solutos – 'we who have been freed'; *solutos* is the perfect participle passive from *solvo*; *culpis* – dative, 'from our faults'

15. fac – imperative, 'make us gentle (*mites*) and chaste (*castos*)'

16. praesta ... para – more imperatives, 'provide (for us) ... prepare (for us) ...'

17. ut ... collaetemur – *ut* + subjunctive (see Appendix): 'so that we can rejoice', the verb is deponent *laetor* strengthened by the suffix *col-*, a common habit in later Latin; *videntes* – present participle from *video*, 'while we are seeing'

18. sit laus – another version of the doxology (compare with the last verse of *Veni Creator Spiritus*)

19. Deo ... Christo ... Spiritui Sancto – all datives (of possession with *sit*); *summum decus* – 'the greatest dignity'

20. tribus – dative agreeing with *Deo*, *Christo* and *Spiritui Sancto*, supply 'who are' with *unus*.

2. *Huc Usque*

This lament from the famous *Carmina Burana* collection (see *Annus Horribilis*, Chapter 13) is in three-line stanzas, with each line having seven syllables. The trochaic rhythm is not quite as clear as in *Ave Maris Stella* – in the first stanza, for example, only the last line is obviously trochaic; nonetheless, the alternation of strong and weak accents thoughout characterises the poem, which was probably intended to be sung anyway (the musical setting would have made the rhythm obvious).

The stanzas rhyme in pairs: aab, ccb, dde, ffe. I have moved the verse beginning *Sum in tristitia* to follow that beginning *Hoc dolorem cumulat*, with the aim of preserving the rhyme scheme without drastically altering the flow of the narrative – usually *Sum in tristitia* is given as the final stanza.

Huc usque has attracted much scholarly comment, with some arguing that it really is the complaint of a pregnant woman abandoned by her lover, some even asserting it is by Heloise herself (for whom, see Chapter 5), while others deny it is anything other than a medieval monkish classroom exercise. Whatever the truth, there's no escaping the poem's air of sincerity – it's easy to feel the poignancy of the girl's awkward situation.

Huc usque, me miseram,
rem bene celaveram,
et amavi callide.

Res mea tandem patuit,
nam venter intumuit,
partus instat gravidae.

Hinc mater me verberat,
hinc pater improperat,
ambo tractant aspere.

Sola domi sedeo,
egredi non audeo,
nec in palam ludere.

Cum foris egredior
a cunctis inspicior
quasi monstrum fuerim.

Cum vident hunc uterum,
alter pulsat alterum,
silent dum transierim.

Semper pulsant cubito,
me designant digito,
ac si mirum fecerim.

Nutibus me indicant,
dignam rogo iudicant,
quod semel peccaverim.

Quid percurram singula?
Ego sum in fabula,
et in ore omnium.

Hoc dolorem cumulat,
quod amicus exsulat
propter illud paululum.

Sum in tristitia
de eius absentia,
in doloris cumulum.

Ob patris saevitiam
recessit in Franciam
a finibus ultimis.

Ex eo vim patior
iam dolore morior,
semper sum in lacrimis.

Notes:

1. huc usque – 'until now'
2. me miseram – Latin puts exclamations into the accusative
3. celaveram – pluperfect, 'I had hidden'
4. bene ... callide – adverbs, 'well ... cunningly'
5. res mea – 'my condition'; *patuit* – 'was exposed'
6. intumuit – 'swelled'
7. partus instat gravidae – 'birth follows pregnancy'; *instare* takes the dative, hence *gravidae*, 'pregnancy'
8. hinc – 'hence', 'for this reason'
9. verberat ... improperat – 'beats ... reproaches'
10. ambo tractant aspere – 'both treat me harshly'
11. domi – locative, 'at home'
12. in palam – *palam* is an adverb, 'openly, publicly', but here with the preposition *in* it is treated as if a noun: 'in public'
13. foris – adverb, 'outdoors'
14. inspicior – passive, 'I am gazed at by all (*a cunctis*)'
15. quasi ... fuerim – 'as if I were ... ', perfect subjunctive of *sum*
16. uterum – accusative of *uterus*, 'womb'
17. alter pulsat alterum – 'one nudges another'
18. dum transierim – 'until I have passed by'; Classical Latin would prefer the indicative after *dum* meaning 'until', but here it is followed by the perfect subjunctive of *transeo* - a late-Latin usage which helps the rhyme
19. cubito ... digito – ablatives, 'with (their) elbow ... finger'; *me designant*, 'they point at me'
20. fecerim – another perfect subjunctive: 'if I had become a marvel'
21. nutibus – 'with their nods'
22. dignam rogo iudicant – accusative + infinitive (see Appendix) with *esse* implied: 'they judge that I am fit for a funeral pyre (*rogo*, ablative of *rogus*)'
23. peccaverim – another rhyming perfect subjunctive, 'because once I had (might have) sinned'
24. quid percurram singula – *percurram*, present subjunctive of *percurro*, '(mentally) run over'; *singula*, neuter, 'each thing'; an echo of Ovid's *singula quid referam* (*Amores* I.5): 'should I go over each thing in turn?'

25. in fabula – 'the subject of gossip', 'the talk of the town'
26. amicus exsulat – her lover has gone into exile because of (*propter*) that trifle (*illud paululum* – diminutive of *paulus*)
27. sum in tristitia – this line has only six syllables, all the others have seven
28. de eius absentia – 'because of his (*eius*) absence'
29. in … cumulum – 'in an increasing amount (of) …'; *cumulus*, 'pile, heap' (English, 'in a heap of trouble')
30. recessit – the *amicus*, who has withdrawn to France because of his father's anger; *a finibus ultimis*, 'from the farthest borders' – does she mean where she lives is on the edge of civilisation? (Abelard felt himself to be just such an exile when he was sent to a monastery in far-flung Brittany)
31. ex eo – 'for this reason'
32. patior … morior – deponents, so active, 'I suffer violence (*vim*) … I am dying from grief (*dolore*, ablative)'
33. in lacrimis – 'in tears' (English, 'lachrymose').

Recommended Listening:

Peter Abelard   *Hymns and Sequences for Heloise*
Schola Gregoriana, Mary Berry
Herald

Cecilia McDowell   *Ave Maris Stella, Christus natus est, Magnificat, A Fancy of Folksong*
Canterbury Chamber Choir, Orchestra Nova, George Vass
Dutton Epoch

Carl Rütti   *Veni Creator Spiritus, Ave Maris Stella* and other works
Cambridge Singers, Ian Moore
Herald

Recommended Reading:

Beeson, C.H. *A Primer of Medieval Latin: An anthology of prose and*
(ed.)   *poetry*
              Catholic University of America Press

Raby, F.J.E. *A History of Christian-Latin Poetry*
               A History of Secular Latin Poetry in the Middle Ages (2 vols)
               Clarendon Press

Waddell, H. *Medieval Latin Lyrics*
(ed.)   Penguin Classics

Beeson's wide-ranging anthology has some notes but no translations. Raby's scholarly books are perhaps for the specialist only. Waddell's attractive collection with English verse translations is sadly out of print but easily found on websites such as abebooks.co.uk or bookfinder.com

CHAPTER 3

VERSE EPITAPHS

As we mentioned in the previous chapter, Latin verse comes in two flavours: accentual verse of the kind we are familiar with from English poetry, and quantitative verse – that is, poetry based on the so-called quantity of syllables (syllabic weight) rather than the natural stress of the words.

On first acquaintance Latin quantitative verse is horribly confusing, so used are we to hearing the metrical rhythm of a line beat time with the stress accents of the words. In quantitative verse, by contrast, the metrical rhythm and the word stress are distinct: whether they coincide or not is up to the discretion of the poet. But it is worth persevering, for not only are the finest works of Classical Latin written in quantitative metre, but such verse occurs frequently on inscriptions and epitaphs.

Take for example two lines of an epitaph inscribed to the memory of Anna Morton née Wortley (d. 1632), from Latimer in Yorkshire:

> *Anna vale longum quae vivens nupta marito*
> *Es bino trino mortua nupta deo.*

We'll work on translating it later, but for now it is enough to observe that this is an example of an elegiac couplet in quantitative metre – famously the metre of Classical love poetry from Catullus to Ovid. Here it is employed in its original mournful context (the sense we still preserve in the English word 'elegy') – as it was used by Catullus in his immortal lines on the death of his brother which end: *atque in perpetuum, frater, ave atque vale*, 'and forever, brother, hail and farewell'.

WHAT IS QUANTITY?

But what do we mean by 'quantitative' verse? Put simply, it is a metrical scheme based on the 'weight' of syllables. Each syllable of a line of verse is regarded as being either heavy or light according to certain fixed rules. It is the specific pattern of heavy and light syllables that determines the metre of the verse.

The earliest Latin poetry written in the old Saturnian metre may or may not have been based on the stress accents of words (scholars continue to debate this issue), but when the Romans encountered Greek culture they were consumed by it. Quintus Ennius (239-169 B.C.) wrote the first Latin epic in hexameters – the metre of Homer's *Iliad* and *Odyssey* – and thereafter all Classical Latin verse used such Greek quantitative metres.

SYLLABLES VS. VOWELS

Unfortunately, older Latin textbooks (and some modern ones) confuse syllable weight with vowel length. This issue was clarified by Professor W. Sidney Allen in his definitive study *Vox Latina* in 1965: syllables have 'weight' (i.e. are either heavy or light) – this being a convention of verse – whereas vowels are either long or short depending on their natural pronunciation. So, for example, the final 'a' of *femina* (nominative) is a short vowel – and it is always pronounced as a short vowel regardless of whether it crops up in prose or poetry. But the final 'a' of *feminā* (ablative) is long – 'aah' – and is always pronounced long.

How do you know if a vowel is long or short? That's no problem, fortunately: dictionaries and grammar books always mark long vowels (e.g. *habeō habēre*); unmarked vowels are therefore short.

In contrast, the metrical weight or quantity of a syllable in a line of verse can vary according to certain complicated rules.

Rules for scansion and determining syllable quantity:

- A <u>light syllable</u> contains a short vowel either on its own or followed by (a) a single consonant or (b) another vowel but without forming a diphthong
- A <u>heavy syllable</u> contains (a) a long vowel (b) a diphthong (c) a vowel (long or short) followed by two consonants: these two consonants may be either in the same word or in two separate words
- If the second consonant of a two-consonant pair is l or r the previous

> syllable if it contains a short vowel can be counted as either light or
> heavy
> • A long vowel always entails a heavy syllable, but a heavy syllable can
>   contain a short vowel (i.e. before two consonants)
> • i and u standing before a vowel in the same syllable are
>   consonants
> • h does not count either as a vowel or consonant
> • u after q is not a separate vowel but forms part of a single (not
>   double) consonant with the q
> • if a word ending in a vowel or m is followed by a word beginning
>   with a vowel or h, the final syllable of the first word is elided: that
>   is it is 'knocked out' and not counted as part of the metre

SCANSION I — THE HEXAMETER

Confused? Let's look again at the first line of the Latimer epitaph:

Anna vale longum quae vivens nupta marito

Scansion is the method of 'scanning' a line of verse in order to indicate
the pattern of syllables which makes up the metrical scheme. Placing
a ⁻ symbol above a syllable in standard scansion notation indicates it
is heavy, whereas a ˘ symbol indicates it is light.

Unfortunately (again) we court more confusion as these are the very
same symbols traditionally used to indicate long and short vowels!
Take a deep breath. To make matters clearer, I have indicated a long
vowel with a ⁻ directly over the relevant letter (all other vowels are
short), and placed the scansion symbols on the line above. Soldiering
on, here is the line scanned:

```
  1      2    3        4      5      6
  ⁻ ˘ ˘ | ⁻ ⁻ | ⁻    ⁻ | ⁻ ˘ | ⁻ ˘  ˘ | ⁻ ⁻
```
Anna valē longum quae vīvens nupta marītō

If we isolate the metrical scheme we get the following:

— ˘ ˘ | — — | — — | — — | — ˘ ˘ |— —

This, it turns out, is the classic hexameter line of Ennius, Virgil and the Latin epic poets, e.g.

I   2   3 4   5   6
— ˘ ˘ | — ˘ ˘ |— —|— — | — ˘ ˘ |— —
Arma virumque canō Trōiae quī prīmus ab ōrīs

'I sing of arms and the man, who first from the shores of Troy ...'
(Virgil, *Aeneid* I.1)

The line is called a hexameter (from the Greek word for six) because it is divided into six metrical 'feet'. Each foot consists of either a dactyl — ˘ ˘ ('dum diddy') or a spondee — — ('dum dum').

It might be helpful to think of these heavy and light syllables as corresponding to musical notes: a heavy — ('dum') syllable is equivalent to a crotchet or full note, while a light ˘ ('di') is equivalent to a quaver or half-note. In music, two quavers occupy the same time as one crotchet; so a heavy — can be thought of as twice the length of a light ˘ (or a 'dum' is twice as long as a 'di'). In hexameter lines, this means that a trochee (— ˘) can be substituted for a dactyl (— ˘ ˘), both occupying one 'foot'.

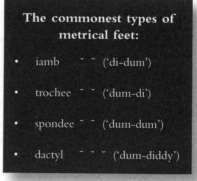

The commonest types of metrical feet:

- iamb   ˘ — ('di-dum')
- trochee — ˘ ('dum-di')
- spondee — — ('dum-dum')
- dactyl — ˘ ˘ ('dum-diddy')

THE CAESURA AND LEONINE RHYME

In Classical Latin poetry, the hexameter conventionally has a division called the *caesura* (from the verb *caedere*, 'to cut') at roughly the mid-way point of the line, usually in the middle of the third foot. This was originally a break in the metrical scheme only, not necessarily a pause in the sense. Sometimes however the *caesura* is reinforced by a sense break, as in Virgil's line quoted above where it occurs after the word *cano*. By medieval times this division had become so definite that it was often marked by rhyme, effectively breaking the hexameter into two separate lines: such an internal rhyme is known as a leonine rhyme.

An example of a rhymed hexameter epitaph from St. Albans Cathedral:

> *Vir Dominī vērus jacet hīc heremīta Rogērus*
> *Et sub eō clārus meritīs heremīta Sigārus.*

> 'A true man of god lies here, the hermit Roger
> And beneath him famous for his services the hermit Sigar.'

Both lines are divided at the *caesura* in the middle of the metrical scheme of each line; this is reinforced by the rhyming of *verus ...* *Rogerus* and *clarus ... Sigarus*.

'SHAVE AND A HAIRCUT' – THE CADENCE

Before we move on to translate some examples, there is one other feature of the hexameter line worth noting. The last two feet of most hexameters form a characteristic cadence consisting of a dactyl (fifth foot) and a spondee (sixth foot), in which the metrical beat and the word stress coincide: 'dum-diddy dum-dum' or, in English, 'shave and a haircut'.

As mentioned above, throughout the rest of the line there is no firm connection between beat and word stress, but this distinctive cadence serves to provide listeners (Latin poetry was always read aloud) with an aural signal that the line has come to end – such was also the function in later times of rhyme. For example, in Virgil's first line of the *Aeneid* we have:

$$5 \qquad\quad 6$$
$$\underline{-} \quad \smile \;\; \smile \;\; | \;\; \underline{-} \; \underline{-}$$

prīmus ab ōrīs

where the natural word stress falls on the first beat of *prīmus* and of *ōrīs*. The Latimer epitaph has exactly the same rhythm:

$$\overset{5}{\bar{-}} \smile \smile \mid \overset{6}{-} -$$

nupta marītō

Where the stress of *marītō* falls on the long ī. The cadence does not have to begin on a new word, as in the rhymed hexameter from St. Albans:

$$\overset{5}{-} \smile \smile \mid \overset{6}{-} -$$

(herem)-īta Rogērus

The long ī in *heremīta* and ē in *Rogērus* are where the word stress falls. This audible cadence helps us to remember that Latin poetry must always be read aloud.

A final note: the very last syllable of each line can be either heavy or light, but for the purpose of the metre it is regarded as being heavy (or at least indeterminate). So the –*us* of *Rogērus* is light, but since it falls at the end of the line it may be regarded as heavy.

HEXAMETER EPITAPHS

1. *From Chicksands Priory, Bedfordshire*

A short epitaph to an unfortunate nun named Rosata, who – so the story goes – was punished for becoming pregnant by being entombed behind a wall in the cloisters. Her ghost is said to appear on 17th of each month.

> *Moribus ornata jacet*
> *hic bona Berta Rosata*

Beneath the Latin text there is an English translation:

> 'By Virtues guarded and by Manners graced
> Here here alas! is fair Rosata placed.'

If we write the line out as a single hexameter, mark the long vowels and then do the scansion we get:

```
     1        2    3        4         5      6
     –  ˘ ˘  |  –  –| –  ˘  ˘  |  –    ˘ ˘  | –  ˘  ˘ | – –
```
Mōribus ornāta jacet (h)īc bona Berta Rosāta.

Here the hexameter is divided into two halves by the leonine rhyme, and unlike a Classical hexameter each half ends with a syllable that can be regarded as metrically indeterminate (i.e. it can be either heavy or light). So the final vowels of both *ornata* and *Rosata* are short, though for the sake of the metrical sceme I have marked both as if they occupy heavy syllables. This is an example of how the importance of rhyme has begun to take precedence over strict scansion, signalling a move away from Classical quantity towards rhymed accentual verse.

Notes:

1. moribus – ablative plural of *mos, mōris*, here 'morals'
2. ornata ... Rosata – adjective and noun; *ornata* is the perfect participle passive from verb *orno, ornare*, 'adorn'
3. jacet hic – 'h' does not count when scanning the metre, so the final syllable of *jacet* is light not heavy
4. bona Berta – the scansion tells us that both *bona* and *Berta* end with short 'a's, hence nominative as we would expect; the first syllable of *Berta* is heavy according to the rule that says a light vowel followed by two consonants makes a heavy syllable
5. I am grateful to Francesca Gurner for providing me with this epitaph. Fascinatingly, exactly the same inscription is also recorded at Jesus College, Cambridge with the date 1261 – which sounds about right for such a two-part rhymed hexameter. Where is the real Berta Rosata buried?

2. 'The Once and Future King'

'Yet some men say in many parts of England that King Arthur is not dead, but had by the will of our Lord Jesu into another place; and men say that he shall come again, and he shall win the holy cross ... But many men say that there is written upon his tomb this verse:

HIC IACET ARTHURUS, REX QUONDAM REXQUE FUTURUS'

(Malory, *Le Morte d'Arthur* Book XXI, Chapter 7)

Scanned:

1 2 3 4 5 6
– ⏑ ⏑ | – – | – – | – – | – ⏑ ⏑ | – –
Hīc iacet Arthūrus, rex quondam rexque futūrus.

Notes:

1. a hexameter line with leonine rhyme (*Arthurus … futurus*)
2. hic – we have already seen two examples of *iacet (h)īc* above; handily for scansion the phrase *hīc iacet* forms a dactyl (so long as the next word begins with a vowel); the 'i' is long in *hīc* meaning 'here' – distinguish from the pronoun *hic* (nominative masculine singular) which has a short 'i'
3. quondam – adverb, 'formerly', 'in ancient times'
4. futurus – future participle of *sum, esse*; in poetry and in later Latin prose, the future participle is often used to express purpose (see Appendix).

3. *From Lavenham, Suffolk*

This curious hexameter epitaph was once to be seen on a monument in the churchyard of St Peter and St Paul's Church in Lavenham. Compare with *Ecclesiastes* I.9: *Quid est quod fuit? ipsum quod futurum est. Quid est quod factum est? ipsum quod faciendum est*, 'The thing that hath been, it is that which shall be; and that which is done is that which shall be done' (King James translation).

Quod fuit esse, quod est, quod non fuit esse, quod esse,
Esse quod est, non esse quod est, non est, erit, esse.

(John Wiles, 1694)

Scanned:

1 2 3 4 5 6
– ⏑ ⏑ | – ⏑ ⏑ | – – | – ⏑ ⏑ | – ⏑ ⏑ | – –
Quod fuit esse, quod est, quod nōn fuit esse, quod esse,

```
  1          2       3        4        5        6
- ˘   ˘  |  -    -| - ˘   ˘  | -   - |  -  ˘ ˘ | - -
```

Esse quod est, nōn esse quod est, nōn est, erit, esse

Notes:

1. quod – *qu*- counts as a single consonant
2. esse – though the first 'e' is short it is followed by two consonants, making the first syllable heavy
3. non – the only long vowel in the couplet is the 'ō' of *nōn*
4. fuit … est … erit – perfect, present and future tenses respectively
5. translation depends entirely on how you decide to take *quod* and *esse*: *quod* can mean 'that (thing) which' (neuter pronoun) or 'because'; *esse* is 'to be' but also '(the state of) being' or 'existing'
6. are we to take it as a riddle: what is it that used to exist but exists no longer in the same state yet still exists in a state of non-existence and will exist again? Answer: the deceased, who is now a corpse but whose soul will live on? Based on this idea, for my tentative translation I take the first *quod* in line 2 as 'because', so I get 'because it is existing', with the 'it' being *non esse quod est*, 'that which is not existing'
7. any number of other interpretations are possible!

4. *From Salisbury Cathedral*

The monument in the nave of Salisbury Cathedral in which this inscription can be seen is usually identified as belonging to Bishop Jocelin, though some authorities ascribe it to St. Osmund, who was Bishop 1078-1099. The sepulchre was originally in Old Sarum before it was moved to the Cathedral in 1226. The inscription is written around the sides of the effigy. Note the lines rhyme in pairs (*ensis … ensis, potentum … nocentum, duxit … reluxit*).

> FLENT HODIE SALESBERIE QUIA DECIDIT ENSIS
> JUSTITIE, PATER ECCLESIAE SALISBERIENSIS.
> DUM VIGUIT, MISEROS ALUIT, FASTUSQUE POTENTUM
> NON TIMUIT, SED CLAVA FUIT TERRORQUE NOCENTUM.

DE DUCIBUS, DE NOBILIBUS PRIMORDIA DUXIT
PRINCIPIBUS PROPE Q:TB' QUASI GEMA RELUXIT.

(?Bishop Jocelin, 1184)

Scanned (first line only):

<pre>
 I   2   3   4   5   6
 -   ˇˇ|- - |-ˇˇ|-ˇˇ | - ˇˇ |- -
</pre>

Flent hodiē Sālesberiē quia dēcidit ensis

Notes:

1. Salesberie – locative: 'at Salisbury'; scansion dictates that the
   first and last vowels are long as they fall in heavy syllables;
   whether the middle 'e' is long or short, it falls in a heavy
   syllable by virtue of being followed by two consonants

2. decidit – distinguish between this verb *dēcido, dēcidere*, 'fall' or
   'die' and *dēcĭdo, decīdere*, 'cut down' or 'decide'

3. Justitie – genitive singular: the final *-e* is medieval Latin for
   the Classical diphthong *–ae*; it qualifies *ensis*, 'the sword of
   Justice'

4. pater – nominative, followed by genitives *ecclesiae Salisberiensis*:
   'the father of the church of Salisbury'; the middle 'e' of *ecclesiae*
   must be short according to the scansion, though a long vowel
   is more usual

5. viguit ... aluit ... non timuit – perfect tenses of *vigere* ('thrive,
   flourish' i.e. while he was alive and active), *alere* ('nourished,
   supported') and *timere* ('fear')

6. fastusque potentum – *fastūs* (long 'u') is accusative plural fourth
   declension, after *non timuit*, of *fastus* (short 'u'), 'haughtiness,
   arrogance'; *potentum* is genitive plural of *potens*, 'powerful'

7. clava – 'a club' or 'cudgel' or a medieval mace; perhaps translate
   as 'scourge'

8. nocentum – genitive plural (like its rhyme *potentum*) of *nocens*,
   'criminal', 'guilty'

9. de Ducibus ... de nobilibus – 'from Dukes ... from nobles'
   (possibly take *Principibus* with *nobilibus*)

10. primordia duxit – 'traced his ancestry'; *primordium*, 'origin,
    source'

11. Principibus ... reluxit – the meaning of this last line depends

on the reading of the odd abbreviation *Q:TB*, which may be the result of a mason's slipshod carving. In 1947, F.J.E. Raby suggested *quis vicibus* – where *quis* is a contraction for ablative *quibus* – while in 1971 H. de S. Shortt suggested *quisque tribus*. The reconstruction in my old copy of *Bell's Cathedral Guide* for Salisbury, *propeque tibi*, cannot be right as it is metrically incorrect (the *Guide* also omits the word *quasi*).

12. Principibus – this could go with Raby's conjectural *quis vicibus* ('like a precious jewel he shone light upon those Princes in turn') or Shortt's *quisque tribus* ('… upon each of the three Princes'), or it could be taken with *nobilibus* from the previous line ('he traced his ancestry from noble Princes')

13. Q:TB – there is no entirely satisfactory solution to expanding this abbreviation. Perhaps *quīque tibi*, where the pronoun *qui* has *–que* added to it: 'and he who shone for you'? The final 'i' of *tibi* can be either short or long, making the syllable either light or heavy; here it would have to be:

$$- \ \smile \smile \mid - \ \smile \ \smile \mid$$

quīque tibī quasi

This suggestion allows us to consider the phrase *prope …
reluxit* as an independent clause

14. quasi gema reluxit – 'he shone forth like a precious jewel'; there is an 'm' missing in the word *gemma*: the double consonant makes the first syllable heavy, thus *gemma reluxit* provides the final two-foot cadence ('shave and a haircut')

15. I am grateful to Suzanne Eward, Librarian of Salisbury Cathedral, for providing me with much useful information about this epitaph.

5. From St. Albans Cathedral

This epitaph is no longer extant, but a photograph of it from 1872 survives; the text is printed along with biographical notes in O'Keefe's *Latin Inscriptions in St. Albans Abbey* (see recommended reading below).

Hic jacet Humphredus Dux ille Glocestrius olim,
Henrici Sexti Protector, fraudis ineptae

Detector, dum ficta notat miracula ceci.
Lumen erat patriae columen venerabile regni.
Pacis amans musisque favens melioribus, unde
Gratum opus Oxonio quae nunc Schola Sacra refulget.
Invida sed mulier, regno regi sibi nequam,
Abstulit hunc humili vix hoc dignata sepulchro.
Invidia rumpente tamen post funera vixit.

(Humphrey, Duke of Gloucester, 1447)

Scanned (first line only):

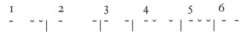

Hīc jacet Humphrēdus Dux ille Glocestrius ōlim

Notes:

1. Humphredus … Dux – the 'h' beginning *Humphredus* does not count for the purposes of scansion; whereas the 'x' in *Dux* counts as a double consonant, so though the 'u' is a short syllable the consonant is heavy

2. ille – this pronoun when used as an adjective to describe someone can be translated as 'the distinguished (person)'

3. Glocestrius – if the second consonant of a consonant pair is 'l' or 'r' the preceding syllable can be regarded as either heavy or light (so long as its vowel is short); in this case we have *Gl-* beginning *Glocestrius* so the preceding *–le* of *ille* can be scanned as light. *Glocestrius* is an adjective agreeing with *Dux*: 'Duke of Gloucester'

4. Henrici Sexti – genitive after *protector*; note the jingle *protector … detector*

5. fraudis ineptae – genitive after *detector*: 'of an inept fraud'

6. ficta … miracula – *ficta* (whence English 'fiction') is the perfect participle of *fingo*, with *miracula* (neuter plural of *miraculum*) – better to translate as singular in English: Humphrey was credited with exposing a man who claimed to have been cured of blindness by having him identify colours, which he should not have been able to do if he really had been blind all his life; *notat* – 'he identified'

7. ceci – genitive, 'of the blind man'; the *-ae* diphthong (here of *caecus*) is regularly shortened to *-e* in medieval Latin

8. columen – figuratively 'a keystone' or 'corner-stone'; adjective *venerabile* (neuter) is in agreement; *regni* is genitive of *regnum*, 'kingdom'

9. amans – present participle of *amo* with the genitive of *pax*: 'fond of peace'

10. favens – 'favourable to', present participle of intransitive verb *faveo* followed by the dative: here *musa* ('muse') is metonymy for 'art' or any study presided over by one of the Muses; *melioribus* – 'nobler' or 'higher'

11. gratum opus Oxonio – 'a work that enjoys favour with Oxford' (*Oxonio*, dative). This is an echo of the (probably spurious) lines which were said to have prefaced Virgil's *Aeneid*: *gratum opus agricolis*, 'a work to win favour with farmers'

12. Schola Sacra – Humphrey contributed books and donations to the Divinity School (completed 1488); *quae refulget* – 'which shines / is resplendent'

13. invida ... mulier – 'a malevolent woman', identified by O'Keefe as Margaret of Anjou, Henry VI's queen who is said to have been responsible for Humphrey's downfall

14. regno regi sibi nequam – 'worthless' (*nequam*) with datives of *regnum*, *rex* and *se*: 'to the kingdom, to the king, (and) to herself'

15. abstulit – perfect tense of *aufero*, 'carry away', here = 'kill' or 'destroy'; *hunc* – accusative of pronoun *hic*, 'him'

16. dignata – perfect participle passive of *digno*, 'consider worthy', feminine because it is the *invida mulier* who did not consider him (Humphrey) worthy of *humili ... hoc ... sepulchro*, ablatives, 'this humble tomb'

17. invidia rumpente – ablative absolute (see Appendix), 'though broken by ill-will' (note the poetical effect of *invida ... invidia*); *rumpente* is the present participle of *rumpo*

18. *funera* – accusative plural of neuter *funus*, 'burial rites' (English 'funeral'), so therefore also 'death'.

SCANSION II – THE PENTAMETER: ELEGIAC COUPLETS

Turning again to the Latimer epitaph we encountered at the beginning of the chapter, we can see that the second line of the couplet is slightly different from the first:

$$\bar{\ } \ \bar{\ }|\bar{\ } \ \bar{\ } \ |\bar{\ }| \ \bar{\ } \ \breve{\ }\breve{\ }| \ \bar{\ } \ \breve{\ } \ \breve{\ }|\bar{\ }$$

Es bīnō trīnō mortua nupta deō

This is the so-called pentameter line, as it consists of five feet in the pattern 2 ½ + 2 ½, i.e.

$$\bar{\ } \ \breve{\ } \ \breve{\ }| \ \bar{\ } \ \breve{\ } \ \breve{\ }|\bar{\ } \quad \text{x 2}$$

In the first half we can replace a dactyl ($\bar{\ } \ \breve{\ } \ \breve{\ }$) with a spondee ($\bar{\ } \ \bar{\ }$), just as with hexameter lines. However, the second half must always contain two dactyls. Pairing a hexameter line and a pentameter line forms an elegiac couplet. In our example, the break in the pentameter at the halfway point (known as *diaresis*) is further emphasised by another leonine rhyme (*trino … deo*).

The elegiac couplet was adopted from Greek models and quickly refined by the Latin love elegists Catullus, Tibullus, Propertius, Sulpicia and Ovid. For example:

(a) hexameter:

$$\overset{1}{\bar{\ }} \ \breve{\ } \ \breve{\ } \ | \overset{2}{\ \bar{\ } \ \breve{\ } \ \breve{\ }} | \overset{3}{\bar{\ }\breve{\ }\breve{\ }} | \overset{4}{\bar{\ } \ \breve{\ } \ \breve{\ }} \ | \overset{5}{\ \bar{\ } \ \breve{\ } \ \breve{\ }} | \overset{6}{\bar{\ } \ \bar{\ }}$$

Arma grauī numerō uiolentaque bella parābam

(b) pentameter:

$$\overset{1}{\bar{\ } \ \breve{\ }\breve{\ }} | \overset{2}{\ \bar{\ } \ \breve{\ }\breve{\ }} | \overset{½}{\bar{\ }} | \overset{3}{\bar{\ } \ \breve{\ } \ \breve{\ }} | \overset{4}{\bar{\ } \ \breve{\ } \ \breve{\ }} \ | \overset{½}{\bar{\ }}$$

edere, materiā conueniente modīs

'I was preparing to tell in solemn measure of arms and violent wars, with the subject-matter agreeing with the metre.'

(*Ovid, Amores* I.1-2)

The couplet is generally felt to be a self-contained unit, thus making it an ideally compact vehicle for pithy epigrams (as the poet Martial knew) or poignant sentiments suitable for epitaphs.

ELEGIAC EPITAPHS

1. *From Latimer, Yorkshire*

> *Anna vale longum quae vivens nupta marito*
> *Es bino trino mortua nupta deo.*

(Anna Morton née Wortley, 1632)

Scanned:

```
 1      2     3      4      5       6
 ‒    ˇ ˇ|‒  ‒ | ‒   ‒  | ‒  ‒ |  ‒   ˇ  ˇ |‒ ‒
```
Anna valē longum quae vīvens nupta marītō

```
 1     2    ½ 3     4      ½
 ‒    ‒|‒  ‒ |‒| ˇ ˇ ˇ| ‒    ˇ ˇ|‒
```
Es bīnō trīnō mortua nupta deō

Notes:

1. Anna vale – see *Annus Horribilis*, Chapter 2 for *vale* and other conversational Latin

2. longum – adverb with *vivens*, 'living long'

3. quae ... nupta – subject of *quae* is *Anna*; *nupta* is the perfect participle of *nubo*, 'marry', so 'having been married' or 'a wife'

4. marito ... bino – dative: 'to a second husband' or 'to a pair of husbands', i.e. she was married twice. *Bini*, 'two each' or 'a pair', is usually plural: here it is singular, presumably to make a nice poetic jingle as well as a contrast: *marito bino ... trino deo*

5. trino ... deo – *trini* (plural) is 'three each' or 'three'; but in the singular it specifically means 'threefold' or 'triple', so here 'a triple god' i.e. the Trinity; literally then, 'you are a wife to a triple god', i.e. you are married a third time to God

6. mortua – nominative (short final 'a', see scansion) perfect participle active of deponent verb *morior*, agreeing with *Anna*, 'having died' or 'dead'

7. For Anna's father, see (5) below.

2. *From Holy Trinity Church, Stratford-upon-Avon*

> *Judicio Pylium, genio Socratem, arte Maronem*
> *Terra tegit, populus maeret, Olympus habet.*
>
> (William Shakespeare, 1616)

Scanned:

```
   1     2     3     4          5          6
 - ˘ ˘| - ˘ ˘| - ˘˘| -    ˘    ˘ | -    ˘    ˘ | - -
```
Judiciō Pylium, geniō Socrat(em), arte Marōnem

```
   1     2     ½  3        4          ½
 - ˘ ˘| -  ˘ ˘ |-| -   ˘   ˘| -   ˘   ˘| -
```
Terra tegit, populus maeret, Olympus habet

Notes:

1. Judicio … genio … arte – ablatives describing Shakespeare: 'in judgement/discernment … in inspiration … in skill'. The translation begins more smoothly if we take the second line first, and then supply a link such as '(he who was) a Nestor in judgement …'

2. Pylium – *Pylius* is an adjective, 'belonging to Pylos', the birthplace of Nestor, thus it also refers to Nestor himself, the wise sage whose advice was invaluable to the Greeks during the Trojan War; the 'y' is a transliteration of the Greek letter υ (*upsilon*), so counts as a (short) vowel

3. Socratem – two points of scansion to notice: firstly, the first

---

The Shakespeare memorial

Judicio Pylium, genio Socratem, arte Maronem
Terra tegit, populus maeret, Olympus habet.
Stay, passenger, why goest thou by so fast?
Read, if thou canst, whom envious death hath placed
Within this monument: Shakespeare, with whom
Quick nature doed; whose name doth deck his tomb
Far more than cost; sith all that he had writ
Leaves living art but page to serve his wit.
Obiit ano doi 1616. Aetatis 53. Die 23 Ap.

(monument erected 1621)

syllable of *Sōcrates* should be heavy, as the 'o' is a long vowel, but here it is incorrectly treated as short; secondly, the final syllable is elided as it ends in *–m* before the next word *arte* which begins with a vowel – this elision means the syllable is not counted

4. Maronem – the full name of the poet we know in English as Virgil was Publius Vergilius Maro

5. tego ... maeret ... habet – all present tense, 'covers ... mourn ... holds'

6. Olympus – like *Pylium*, the 'y' here = Greek *upsilon* so a (short) vowel, but the syllable is heavy because followed by two consonants; the word is an appropriate substitute for the Christian heaven in the context of an epitaph invoking Shakespeare's Greek and Roman counterparts.

3. *From Gloucester Cathedral*

This poignant couplet is inscribed on a brass plaque on the floor of the Lady Chapel:

> *Parve, nec invideo, sine me, puer, ibis ad astra,*
> *Parve, nec invideas, laetus ad astra sequar.*
>
> (Charles Sutton, aged seven days)

Scanned:

```
   1        2      3    4       5      6
  -  ˘   ˘  |-  ˘˘|-˘˘|  -    ˘˘| -˘˘ | --
```
Parve, nec invideō, sine mē, puer, ībis ad astra,

```
   1        2     ½  3        4       ½
  -  ˘  ˘|  -˘˘|-|  -  ˘   ˘|- ˘  ˘| -
```
Parve, nec invideās, laetus ad astra sequar

Notes:

1. the first line is modelled on *Ovid's Tristia*, Book I line 1: *Parve, nec invideo, sine me, liber, ibis in urbem*, 'Little book, I begrudge it not, you will go to the city without me', substituting vocative *puer* for *liber* and *ad astra* for *in urbem*. The pentameter touchingly expands the sentiment

2. invideas – present subjunctive of *invideo* which is intransitive so does not take a direct object: 'may you not begrudge it',

 or simply, 'do not begrudge it'

3. laetus − translate as adverb, 'happily'

4. sequar − future tense of *sequor*, 'I will follow (you)'; the present subjunctive is also *sequar*, but the sense seems to be future.

4. *From St. Albans Cathedral*

> *Condita quae iacet hoc Mulier sub marmore, uixit*
> *Uxor, Amica, parens Candida, Iusta, pia,*
> *Hei mihi quod Vivo, quo non licet Ire, Marito.*
> *Mors sibi Vita Fuit, Vivere Morsque Mihi.*

(Alice Ramridge, 1710)

Scanned (first couplet only):

```
  1      2        3       4     5       6
  − ˘ ˘| −   ˘ ˘| −    ˘ ˘|− − | −   ˘ ˘| − −
```
Condita quae iacet hōc Mulier sub marmore, uīxit

```
  1      2        ½  3       4     ½
  − ˘  ˘| − ˘  ˘|− |  −    ˘ ˘| − ˘  ˘|−
```
Uxor, Amīca, parens Candida, Iusta, pia

Notes:

1. the words are actually inscribed in half-lines: *Condita quae iacet hoc / Mulier sub marmore, vixit*; line 3 is another example of a leonine rhyme (*Vivo ... Marito*)

2. condita − perfect participle passive from *condo*, which can mean 'found, establish' but also 'bury, inter'

3. uxor ... pia − the second line is a string of epithets describing the *mulier*

4. hei mihi − 'alas for me!'; *quod* = 'because'

5. vivo ... marito − dative after impersonal verb *non licet*: 'a living husband is not allowed'

6. quo non licet ire − *quo* is an adverb, 'in that place to which'

7. sibi ... mihi − 'for her ... for me'

8. Mors − the final couplet is nicely balanced, observe the alliterative effect of *mors ... morsque mihi* and *vita ... vivere:* supply *est* in the final clause, 'to live (or living) is death for me'.

5. From St. George's Chapel, Windsor

HIC WORTLEIE TVIS DOLOR, ET DECVS OMNE RECVMBIS,
PLEBIS HONOS, EQVITVM GLORIA, REGIS AMOR.
QVI QVOD ERAS PATRIE BONVS, ORBI CHARVS, EGENIS
VTILIS, HI PARITER TE CECIDISSE DOLENT.
VERVM, QVANDO FIDES, PIETAS, CONSTANCIA, VIRTVS,
INVENIET SIMILEM, RELIGIOSA VIRVM
INVENIRE QVIDEM SIMILEM, SED DISPARE SEXV:
SIC VXOR SIMILIS, DISSIMVLISQ. TIBI.

(Sir Richard Wortley, 1603)

Scanned (first couplet only):

1	2	3	4	5	6

–   – |– ˘ ˘|–   ˘ ˘| –   ˘ ˘ | – ˘   ˘ | – –

Hīc Wortlēie tuīs dolor, et decus omne recumbis,

1	2	½	3	4	½

– ˘ ˘|– ˘ ˘| – | – ˘ ˘|– ˘ ˘|–

Plēbis honōs, equitum gloria, rēgis amor.

Notes:

1. the father of the Anna commemorated in the elegiac epitaph from Latimer (1) above
2. Wortleie – vocative after *hic recumbis*, 'here you lie'
3. tuis dolor – 'a (source of) grief to yours', i.e. your family
4. decus omne – perhaps better to translate *omne* here as an adverb, 'wholly virtuous'
5. honos ... gloria ... amor – 'the honour (of) ... the glory (of) ... beloved (of)' so all accompanied by genitives: *plebis, equitum, regis*
6. qui ... eras – 'you who were', with *quod*, 'because'
7. patrie – dative, 'to your native country': the medieval *-e* for the Classical *-ae*; *bonus* here means 'loyal (to)'
8. orbi ... egenis – also datives after *c(h)arus* and *utilis*: 'dear to the world, helpful to the needy'
9. hi ... dolent – 'they grieve' then accusative + infinitive (see Appendix), 'that you have died'; *pariter* is the adverb, 'equally, together'
10. verum – introduces a new clause, 'but ...'

11. quando ... inveniet – a question with the verb in the future tense: 'when will x (nominative) find y (accusative)?', the 'x' being a sequence of qualities all qualified by the adjective *religiosa*, the 'y' being *similem virum*

12. invenire – this must be a mistake for *invēnēre*, 'they have found', the contracted third-person plural perfect tense of *invenio*; the present infinitive *invenīre* scans as heavy – light – heavy – light, making it inadmissable in a hexameter line

13. quidem – 'indeed'

14. dispare sexu – ablative, 'from a/the different sex'

15. sic – 'thus', 'so' or 'to such an extent'

16. dissimulisq. – a misspelling for *dissimilis*; the enclitic *–que* is abbreviated as usual.

A HENDECASYLLABIC EPITAPH

The hendecasyllable is a Classical verse metre consisting of 11 syllables per line. It was much used by Catullus (*c.*84-54 B.C.) for light and occasional verse. He famously employed hendecasyllables for two poems about 'my sweetheart's pet sparrow' (*passer deliciae meae puellae*, Poem 2), though some scholars argue that what Catullus in fact meant by his 'sparrow' was something rather ruder, and that the sparrow's death which he eloquently mourns in Poem 3 (*passer mortuus est meae puellae*) is actually a joke about impotence! Blissfully unaware of any such *double entendre*, the following inscription from a marble plaque found at Auch, France in the second century A.D. is inspired by Catullus.

The metrical scheme is 11 syllables in five feet: spondee (or iamb) – dactyl – trochee – trochee – spondee (final syllable can be either heavy or light), i.e.

Epitaph on a pet dog

> *Quam dulcis fuit ista, quam benigna,*
> *Quae cum viveret, in sinu iacebat*
> *Somni conscia semper et cubilis.*
> *O factum male, Myia, quod peristi.*

Latrares modo, si quis adcubaret
Rivalis dominae, licentiosa.
O factum male, Myia, quod peristi.
Altum iam tenet insciam sepulcrum,
Nec sevire potes nec insilire,
Nec blandis mihi morsibus renides.

Scanned (first line only):

$$\bar{} \quad \bar{} | \bar{} \smile \smile | \smile \smile | \bar{} \quad \smile | \bar{} \quad \bar{}$$

Quam dulcis fuit ista, quam benigna

Notes:

1. quam – exclamation, 'how ...'
2. ista – 'that (female) dog'
3. cum viveret – *cum* + subjunctive, 'while she lived'
4. in sinu iacebat – 'lay in my lap'; this echoes the first Catullus *passer* poem: *quem in sinu tenere* (2.2)
5. conscia – adjective *conscius*, 'sharing in' here takes the genitives of *somnus*, 'sleep' and *cubile*, 'bed'
6. o factum male – 'oh, it is badly done!', a direct quote from Catullus' poem on the death of the sparrow: *o factum male, o miselle passer!* (3.16)
7. Myia – the dog's name, from the Greek μυια, 'fly' or 'midge' (Latin *musca*); it scans as a trochee, heavy-light
8. latrares ... adcubaret – imperfect subjunctives: 'you would only bark if any rival (*quis rivalis*) would lay down beside your mistress unrestrained (*licentiosa*)'; *adcubo, adcubare* is followed by the dative, hence *dominae*
9. quod peristi – *quod* = 'because' or 'that'; *peristi* – perfect tense of *pereo* (English 'perish')
10. altum ... sepulcrum – *altus* can mean 'high' or, as here, 'deep'; neuter *sepulcrum* is the subject of the verb *tenet*, 'holds'
11. insciam – accusative, 'unaware', referring to the dog
12. sevire ... insilire – infinitives after *nec potes*: *sevire* is a variant spelling of *saevire*, 'behave ferociously' or 'growl'; *insilire*, 'jump'
13. blandis ... morsibus – ablative; *morsus* (fourth declension) is 'a bite', but taken with *blandus* better to translate 'with affectionate nips'

14. renides – *renideo* can mean 'gleam' or 'reflect' but also 'smile back at' or 'beam' in the same sense as English 'a beaming grin'; the verb is intransitive, so the object is dative *mihi*.

See Chapter 7 for more poetry, including a modern hendecasyllabic poem about another (living!) dog.

Recommended Reading:

Allen, W.S.   *Vox Latina*
Cambridge University Press

The classic study of Classical Latin pronunciation, word stress and syllable quantity.

Betts, G. &   *Beginning Latin Poetry Reader*
Franklin, D.   McGraw Hill

A modern student textbook of Classical verse selections, with helpful grammar notes and translations.

Brooks, C.   *Reading Latin Poetry Aloud*
Cambridge University Press

An excellent collection of Classical, medieval and Neo-Latin verse with full phonetic transcriptions, accompanied by two CDs of the author's reading.

Bond, S.M.   *The Monuments of St. George's Chapel, Windsor*
Oxley & Son

O'Keefe, P.   'Latin Inscriptions in St. Albans Abbey'
The Fraternity of the Friends of Saint Albans Abbey, Occasional Paper No. 7

Two excellent collections of epitaphs, with notes and translations.

CHAPTER 4

CLASSICAL LETTERS

In this and the next chapter we follow an unbroken tradition of Latin letter-writing from antiquity to the eighteenth century. This form of literature could be said to begin and end with Cicero, whose voluminous correspondence with all the leading men of his day remains the paradigm of Latin epistolary style.

I have chosen two examples from Cicero's personal correspondence with his wife Terentia. These are of quite a different character from his letters to statesmen on weighty matters of war and peace. They reveal a steep decline in the relationship between husband and wife: the earliest letter, dating from the period of his exile in 58 B.C., is long and full of affection for the woman who is managing his affairs during his enforced absence from Rome. Thereafter his letters become shorter and shorter, until by 47 B.C. his final note is curt to the point of rudeness. He divorced her in 46 B.C.

1. *Cicero to Terentia*

TULLIUS S.D. TERENTIAE SUAE, TULLIOLAE SUAE, CICERONI SUO
Incohata Thessalonicae, finita Dyrrachi, A.U.C. 696

Et litteris multorum et sermone omnium perfertur ad me, incredibilem tuam virtutem et fortitudinem esse teque nec animi, neque corporis laboribus defatigari. Me miserum! te, ista virtute, fide, probitate, humanitate, in tantas aerumnas propter me incidisse! Tulliolamque nostram, ex quo patre tantas voluptates capiebat, ex eo tantos percipere luctus! Nam quid ego de Cicerone dicam? qui cum primum sapere coepit, acerbissimos dolores miseriasque percepit. Quae si, ut tu scribis, fato facta putarem, ferrem paullo facilius; sed omnia sunt mea culpa commissa, qui ab iis me amari putabam, qui invidebant, eos non sequebar, qui petebant ...

Fac valeas et ad me tabellarios mittos, ut sciam, quid agatur, et vos quid agatis. Mihi omnino iam brevis exspectatio est. Tulliolae et Ciceroni salutem dic. Valete. a.d. VI. Kalendas Decembres Dyrrachi.

(*Epistulae ad Familiares*, XIV.I)

Notes:

1. Tullius – Cicero's full name was Marcus Tullius Cicero (for Roman names, see *Annus Horribilis*, Ch. 5)

2. S.D. – *salutem dicit*, the standard greeting

3. Terentiae ... Tulliolae ... Ciceroni – datives of the addressees; *Tulliola* is an affectionate diminutive of *Tullia*, *Cicero* is his son; *suae ... suo* – 'his dear'

4. incohata ... finita – perfect passive participles (with *epistula* understood) from *incoho*, 'begin' and *finio*, 'finish'

5. Thessalonicae ... Dyrrachi – locatives; exiled by a motion of his arch-enemy Clodius, Cicero went to stay with his friend Plancius in Thessalonica in Macedonia; he has travelled from there to Dyrrachium (in modern Albania) because it is the closest point to Italy (*proxima Italiae* he says later in the letter)

6. A.U.C. 696 – *anno urbis conditae* = 58 B.C.; Romans gave years from the supposed date of the founding of the city of Rome in 753 B.C.; for more on Roman dates see *Annus Horribilis*, Ch. 5

7. et ... et – 'both ... and'

8. multorum ... omnium – by their letters and conversation many people are informing Cicero about Terentia's activities on his behalf

9. perfertur – passive, 'it is reported to me that ...'

10. incredibilem ... esse – accusative + infinitive (see Appendix)

11. te ... defatigari – another accusative + passive infinitive following *perfertur*

12. neque ... neque – 'neither ... nor'; but genitives *animi ... corporis* after *laboribus*: 'you are not exhausted either by the labours of mind or body'

13. me miserum – Latin puts such exclamations into the accusative

14. te ... incidisse – accusative + perfect infinitive: 'that you have fallen'

15. ista – 'a woman well-known for her ...', followed by a list of descriptive ablatives

16. tantas aerumnas – 'such afflictions, troubles'; *propter me*, 'on my account'

17. Tulliolamque ... percipere – another accusative + infinitive after *me miserum*: 'and that our little Tullia ... derives'

18. ex quo patre ... ex eo – 'from her father ... from him'

19. capiebat – the imperfect of *capio*, here meaning 'used to take'

20. voluptates ... luctus – accusative plurals, 'pleasure ... grief'

21. dicam – subjunctive: 'what can I say?'

22. cum primum – 'as soon as'; *sapere* – 'to have understanding, be intelligent'

23. acerbissimos – superlative of *acerbus*, 'bitter' (English: 'acerbic')

24. percepit – perfect tense, 'has perceived, apprehended'

25. quae – refers to his 'sorrows and afflictions'

26. ut scribis – Terentia's opinion in a previous letter

27. fato facta – 'have been made by fate'

28. putarem ... ferrem – imperfect subjunctives, 'I should consider ... I should bear'

29. paullo facilius – adverb *paullo*, 'a little', comparative adverb *facilius*, 'more easily'

30. commissa – perfect participle passive of *committo*, agreeing with *omnia*: 'everything has been brought about'

31. me ... amari – accusative + infinitive after *putabam*: 'that I was loved'

32. qui invidebant ... qui petebant – 'those who were jealous of me ... those who sought me out (as a friend)'; Cicero bemoans the fact that he turned away from those who could help him

33. fac valeas – imperative of *facio* + subjunctive of *valeo*: 'see to it that you keep well'

34. tabellarios – couriers to carry letters

35. ut sciam – *ut* + subjunctive (see Appendix), 'so that I know'; *quid agatur* – passive of *ago*, 'what is being done'; *quid agatis* – 'what you (plural) are doing'

36. mihi ... est – dative of possession: 'I have a short wait (*brevis exspectatio*)'; *omnino* – 'at any rate'
37. dic salutem – imperative: 'give my regards to ...'
38. a.d.VI. Kalendas – i.e. November 25th; the Romans dated days of the month by counting backwards from three key days: the Kalends (1st), Nones (5th or 7th) and the Ides (13th or 15th); for more on Roman dates see *Annus Horribilis*, Ch. 5.

2. Cicero to Terentia

M.T.C.S.P.D. TERENTIAE SUAE
Venusiae, A.U.C. 707

In Tusculanum nos venturos putamus aut Nonis aut postridie. Ibi ut sint omnia parata. Plures enim fortasse nobiscum erunt, et, ut arbitror, diutius ibi commorabimur. Labrum si in balineo non est, ut sit. Item cetera, quae sunt ad victum et ad valetudinem necessaria. Vale. Kal. Octobr. de Venusino.

(*Epistulae ad Familiares*, XIV.XX)

Notes:
1. M.T.C – Marcus Tullis Cicero
2. S.P.D. – the traditional opening, *salutem plurimam dicit*, 'says many a greeting'; *Terentiae* – dative of the addressee
3. Venusiae – locative (modern Venosa)
4. 707 A.U.C. = 47 B.C., see *Annus Horribilis*, Ch. 5
5. Tusculanum – Cicero had a country villa in Tusculum a few miles outside of Rome
6. *nos venturos* – understand *esse* with *venturos* to form an accusative + future infinitive (see Appendix) after *putamus*, plural but referring to himself (the 'royal' we): 'I think that I will arrive ...'
7. Nonis – 'on the Nones', see *Annus Horribilis*, Ch. 5
8. sint ... parata – subjunctive, 'let everything be made ready (perfect passive participle from *paro*)'
9. plures – 'many people'; *erunt* – future tense
10. ut arbitror – deponent, 'as I imagine'
11. diutius – comparative form of adverb *diu*: 'for a considerable time'; *commorabimur* – future tense of *commoror*, 'remain'
12. labrum – 'a wash-basin' for use in the *balineum*, 'bathroom'

13. ut sit – an extremely terse command: 'see to it that there is one'
14. item cetera – 'the same goes for everything else'
15. ad victum … ad valetudinem – after *sunt necessaria*, 'for sustenance … good health'
16. Kal. Octobr. – see *Annus Horribilis*, Ch. 5
17. de Venusino – 'from the district of Venusia'
18. 'A gentleman would write a more civil letter to his housekeeper' (Long).

The next three selections are all quoted verbatim by the biographer Suetonius in his *De Vita Caesarum*, 'Lives of the Caesars', a collection of biographies of the first twelve Caesars which not only provides much invaluable historical information but also makes for a cracking good read.

3. Mark Antony to Octavian

At the best of times the alliance between Caesar's former deputy Mark Antony and his adopted heir Octavian was precarious. After Antony scandalised all Rome by taking up with Cleopatra while remaining married to Octavian's sister Octavia, the breach between the two men became irreparable. After Octavian had publicly attacked Antony for his conduct at the beginning of 33 B.C., Antony replied in this laddish letter, in which he takes his former colleague to task for hypocrisy: 'so what if I'm sleeping with the Queen, I bet you're in bed with one of your many girlfriends as you read this.' In contrast to Antony, the future Augustus was always careful to conceal his own vices behind a semblance of decency.

Quid te mutavit? Quod reginam ineo? Uxor mea est? Nunc coepi, an abhinc annos novem? Tu deinde solam Drusillam inis? Ita valeas, uti tu, hanc epistulam cum leges, non inieris Tertullam aut Terentillam aut Rufillam aut Salviam Titiseniam aut omnes. An refert, ubi et in qua arrigas?

(Suetonius, *Divus Augustus* 69.2)

Notes:

1. quid te mutavit – 'What has changed your mind?' Antony is puzzled about Octavian's apparent change of heart, not yet

realising that his young rival is manipulating Roman public opinion against him

2. quod – 'Is it because …?'
3. ineo – the Oxford Latin Dictionary gives for *ineo*, 'to cover, mount (also applied to human copulation)'; clearly a more colloquial word is called for here, and English has plenty of Anglo-Saxonisms to choose from
4. uxor mea est – another rhetorical question: 'so what, she's not my wife, just a mistress'
5. nunc coepi – 'it's not as if I've begun something new, I started nine years ago (*abhinc annos novem*)'
6. Drusillam – Octavian's first wife; *deinde* – 'well, in that case then …'
7. ita … uti – literally, 'in the same way … as'; *uti* is an alternate form of *ut*: translate as 'you're doing well (*valeas*, literally: 'may you be well') if …'
8. leges – future tense, followed by *inieris* which is future perfect, literally: 'when you will read this … if you will not have been shagging …'
9. Tertullam … Salviam Titiseniam – the names of (some of) Octavian's mistresses
10. an refert – 'what difference does it make?' *refert* is an impersonal verb
11. arrigas – subjunctive in an indirect question; *arrigo*, 'become sexually excited, have an erection' (Oxford Latin Dictionary), again a suitable colloquialism should be supplied.

4. *Augustus to Tiberius*

In later life Augustus corresponded frequently with his family on matters both serious and trivial. This chatty letter about a day spent gambling is addressed to his son-in-law, the future Emperor Tiberius.

Nos, mi Tiberi, quinquatrus satis iucunde egimus; lusimus enim per omnis dies forumque aleatorium calfecimus. Frater tuus magnis clamoribus rem gessit; ad summam tamen perdidit non multum, sed ex magnis detrimentis praeter spem paulatim retractum est. Ego perdidi viginti milia nummum meo nomine, sed cum effuse in lusu liberalis fuissem, ut soleo plerumque. Nam si quas manus remisi cuique exegissem, aut retinuissem quod cuique donavi, vicissem

*vel quinquaginta milia. Sed hoc malo; benignitas enim mea me ad caelestem
gloriam efferet.*

(Suetonius, *Divus Augustus* 71.3)

Notes:

1. mi Tiberi – vocative, 'my dear Tiberius'
2. quinquatrus – a festival of Minerva which lasted five days,
   19th-23rd March
3. satis iucunde egimus – 'we spent … pleasantly enough'; *egimus*
   is perfect tense of *ago*
4. lusimus – perfect tense from *ludo*, 'play'
5. per omnis dies – accusative plural (*omnis* = *omnes*), the
   accusative denoting duration of time: 'throughout every day'
   or 'all day long'
6. forumque aleatorium – *forum* here could mean 'market-place'
   as usual, or refer to the actual gaming-board of the gamblers
   (the *aleatores*); *calfecimus* – perfect tense of *calefacio*, 'make hot,
   keep warm'
7. frater tuus – Drusus, the father of the future Emperor
   Claudius
8. magnis clamoribus – 'amidst great applause', an appreciative
   crowd was watching; *rem gessit* – 'transacted' or 'carried out
   his business'
9. ad summam – 'to sum up', 'in short'
10. perdidit – perfect tense from *perdo*, 'lose'
11. ex magnis detrimentis – 'from a great loss'; *praeter spem* –
    'beyond hope' or 'surpassing hope', i.e. he got lucky
12. paulatim – adverb, 'by degrees', 'gradually'
13. retractum est – perfect passive of *retraho*, 'win back', i.e. his
    loss (*detrimentum*) was clawed back
14. nummum – the genitive plural of *nummus* after *milia* is
    nummum (not *nummorum*)
15. cum … fuissem – *cum* + perfect subjunctive, 'since/after I had
    been …'; *effuse … liberalis* – 'effusively generous'
16. ut soleo plerumque – 'as I am generally accustomed', i.e. 'as
    is my wont'
17. manus – accusative plural (hence *quas*), 'stakes'; *remisi* – perfect
    tense of *remitto*: 'for if I waived those stakes which…'
18. exegissem – pluperfect subjunctive from *exigo*: ' … I had

demanded/called for from each player (*cuique*, dative of *quisque*)'

19. retinuissem – pluperfect subjunctive of *retineo*: 'I had retained what (*quod*) I gave (*donavi*) to each'

20. vicissem – pluperfect subjunctive of *vinco*: 'I would have won'; *vel* – 'perhaps'. Following a main clause in the perfect tense, Latin expresses a completed action with the pluperfect subjunctive.

21. efferet – imperfect subjunctive of *effero*: 'my kindness shall lift me up'.

5. *Augustus to Livia*

The man named Tiberius mentioned in this short note from Augustus to his wife Livia is not Livia's son Tiberius but her grandson from her first marriage, Tiberius Claudius Drusus Nero Germanicus – the future emperor known to us as Claudius, whose stammering, facial tics and other physical disabilities made him an object of derision amongst his family (modern scholarship suggests he may have suffered from cerebral palsy). However Augustus suspected there was more to the boy than his unprepossessing appearance suggested.

Tiberium nepotem tuum placere mihi declamantem potuisse, peream nisi, mea Livia, admiror. Nam qui tam ασαφως loquatur, qui possit cum declam σαφως dicere quae dicenda sunt, non video.

(Suetonius, *Divus Claudius* 4.6)

Notes:

1. Tiberium … potuisse – accusative + infinitive (see Appendix) after *admiror*: 'I'm astonished that Tiberius … was able to please me (*placere mihi*)'; *nepos* can be either 'nephew' (English, 'nepotism') or, as here, 'grandson'

2. declamentem – present participle of *declamo*, 'while declaiming': Claudius had been successful in reciting a pre-prepared speech; by contrast he found speaking *extempore* virtually impossible due to his stutter

3. peream nisi – a real flavour of Augustus' everyday speech: 'let me die unless …' or 'I'll be damned if …'

4. mea Livia – the traditional endearment, 'my dear Livia'

5. qui ... qui – the first *qui* is the pronoun, 'he who speaks so
    ... ; the second *qui* is 'how he is able ...'
6. loquatur ... possit – subjunctives of *loquor* and *possum*; both
    are subjunctive because this is an indirect question after *non
    video*: 'I don't see how he ...' (the direct question would be:
    'How can he ...?')
7. ασαφως ... σαφως – 'obscurely ... clearly'; like many educated
    Romans, Augustus was in the habit of dropping Greek words
    and phrases into his letters, rather as English writers in days
    gone by would do with French (or Latin)
8. quae dicenda sunt – *dicenda* is the gerundive (see Appendix)
    from *dico*, 'I say' agreeing with *quae*: 'those things which need
    to be said'.

The letters exchanged by the younger Pliny (61-*c*.113) and the Emperor
Trajan were published posthumously (possibly by his friend Suetonius)
as the tenth book of Pliny's correspondence. In the year A.D. III Pliny
was sent by Trajan to govern the far-flung province of Bithynia and
Pontus, and many letters relating to provincial administration passed
between them.

6. *Trajan to Pliny*

In this famous letter, the Emperor responds to a question Pliny has
asked him about how to treat those who profess Christianity.

Traianus Plinio.
Actum quem debuisti, mi Secunde, in excutiendis causis eorum, qui Christiani
ad te delati fuerant, secutus es. Neque enim in universum aliquid, quod quasi
certam formam habeat, constitui potest. Conquirendi non sunt; si deferantur et
arguantur, puniendi sunt, ita tamen ut, qui negaverit se Christianum esse idque
re ipsa manifestum fecerit, id est supplicando dis nostris, quamvis suspectus
in praeteritum, veniam ex paenitentia impetret. Sine auctore vero propositi
libelli in nullo crimine locum habere debent. Nam et pessimi exempli nec
nostri saeculi est.

(*Letters*, X.XCVII)

Notes:
1. Plinio – dative of the addressee
2. actum – accusative of *actus*, the perfect participle passive of

ago, here meaning 'method'; *quem debuisti* – perfect tense of *debeo*, 'which you were obliged to'

3. mi Secunde – vocative, the traditional endearment; Pliny's full name was Gaius Plinius Secundus

4. excutiendis – gerundive (see Appendix) of *excutio*, here meaning 'examine, scrutinise', with noun *causis*, literally: 'in the cases which were to be examined'

5. eorum qui – 'of those (people) who ...'

6. delati – the perfect passive participle of *defero*, here 'denounced' or 'reported'

7. neque enim – 'for ... not'; the negative with *aliquid*, 'something', = 'nothing'

8. in universum – 'universally'

9. quod ... habeat – 'which (neuter after *aliquid*) might be regarded (*habeat*) as a fixed arrangement (*certam formam*)'

10. constitui – passive infinitive, in a legal context = 'to be laid down', i.e. no general law can be established

11. conquirendi ... sunt – gerundive + *esse* (see Appendix) of *conquiro*, 'hunt down'

12. deferantur ... arguantur – passive subjunctives of *defero*, 'bring' and *arguo*, 'accuse' – subjunctive because we are dealing with a hypothetical situation

13. puniendi sunt – another gerundive + *esse* (see Appendix) of *punio*, 'punish' (English, 'punitive')

14. ut ... impetret – *ut* + subjunctive (see Appendix), 'let him obtain a pardon (*veniam*) as a result of his repentance (*ex paenitentia*)'; the words *qui negaverit ... in praeteritum* form a parenthesis

15. qui negaverit – accusative + infinitive (see Appendix): 'anyone (*qui*) who will have denied (*negaverit*, future perfect) that he is a Christian'

16. idque ... manifestum fecerit – 'and will have made that plain'

17. re ipsa – 'in fact'

18. supplicando – gerund (see Appendix) of *supplico*: 'by making offerings (to)' + dative *dis nostris*, 'our gods'

19. quamvis ... in praeteritum – 'although having been suspected (perfect participle passive of *suspicio*) in the past'

20. propositi libelli – perfect participle passive of *propono*, literally: 'defamatory pamphlets which have been published' (English,

'libel'), *sine auctore vero* – 'without a genuine author', i.e. anonymously

21. nullo crimine locum habere – literally: 'to have a place in no accusation', i.e. 'have no place in an accusation'

22. pessimi exempli – a characterising genitive after *est*, 'it is characteristic of the worst (kind of) precedent'; *nostri saeculi* – also genitive, 'our present time', he means such anonymous pamphlets do not fit with the open, law-abiding spirit of his reign.

Recommended Reading:

Cicero (trans. Glynn Williams)   ***Letters to His Friends*** (3 vols)
Loeb Classical Library

Pliny (trans. Radice)   ***Letters***
Loeb Classical Library

The Loeb editions have the Latin text and English translation on facing pages.

Suetonius (ed. Carter)   ***Divus Augustus***
Bristol Classical Press

Suetonius (ed. Hurley)   ***Divus Claudius***
Cambridge University Press

Latin texts with notes and commentary.

Suetonius (trans. Graves)   ***The Twelve Caesars***
Folio Society

Robert Graves' classic translation of all the lives.

CHAPTER 5

LATER LETTERS

The art of Latin letter-writing was continued through the Middle Ages. Then, after Petrarch reintroduced the Classical epistolary style of Cicero in the fourteenth century, it positively flourished. As late as the eighteenth century it was the norm for educated men across Europe to correspond in Latin.

1. Heloise (c.1100-1163) to Abelard

The story of the ardent love affair between fiery philosopher Peter Abelard (see Chapter 2) and his brilliant young student Heloise has been preserved in their remarkable letters to each other: Abelard's autobiographical *Historia Calamitatum* ('Story Of My Misfortunes') tells how he was asked to tutor the remarkable young girl at her uncle's home in Paris, how their lessons soon turned into passionate love-making sessions, how Heloise's uncle discovered their affair and how Abelard attempted to placate him by marrying Heloise. But in vain: the uncle's hired thugs attacked Abelard one night and violently castrated him. Thereafter he willingly sought monastic retreat; Heloise, with all her passion intact, was more reluctantly compelled to undertake the same religious (and celibate) life.

Abelard's troubles continued thereafter, as he never could cease engaging in bitter philosophical and doctrinal disputes with his peers. Meanwhile Heloise seemed resigned to her devotional life, and became Abbess of the Paraclete, the monastery Abelard himself had founded. It was there, many years after they had last met, that Abelard's self-pitying *Historia* came into her hands, and prompted the beginning of an exchange of letters between the two.

In these extracts from her first letter to Abelard, Heloise reminds him of how much she has sacrificed for him:

> *Domino suo immo patri, coniugi suo immo fratri, ancilla sua immo filia, ipsius uxor immo soror: Abaelardo Heloisa.*

Missam ad amicum pro consolatione epistolam, dilectissime, vestram ad me forte quidam nuper attulit. Quam ex ipsa statim tituli fronte vestram esse considerans, tanto ardentius eam coepi legere, quanto scriptorem ipsum carius amplector ut, cuius rem perdidi, verbis saltem tamquam eius quadam imagine recreer. Erant memini huius epistolae fere omnia felle et absinthio plena quae scilicet nostrae conversionis miserabilem historiam et tuas, unice, cruces assiduas referebant ...

Nihil umquam Deus scit in te nisi te requisivi, te pure non tua concupiscens. Non matrimonii foedera, non dotes aliquas expectavi, non denique meas voluptates aut voluntates sed tuas, sicut ipse nosti adimplere studui. Et si uxoris nomen sanctius ac validius videtur, dulcius mihi semper exstitit amicae vocabulum aut, si non indigneris, concubinae uel scorti ut quo me videlicet pro te amplius humiliarem, ampliorem apud te consequerer gratiam et sic etiam excellentiae tuae gloriam minus laederem ...

Per ipsum itaque cui te obtulisti Deum te obsecro, ut quo modo potes, tuam mihi praesentiam reddas, consolationem uidelicet mihi aliquam rescribendo hoc saltem pacto ut sic recreata divino alacrior vacem obsequio. Cum me ad turpes olim voluptates expeteres, crebris me epistolis visitabas, frequenti carmine tuam in ore omnium Heloisam ponebas. Me plateae omnes, me domus singulae resonabant. Quanto autem rectius me nunc in Deum quam tunc in libidinem excitares? Perpende, obsecro, quae debes, attende quae postulo et longam epistolam breui fine concludo: Vale unice.

Notes:

1. Domino suo – dative of the addressee, 'to her master', followed by an extraordinary sequence of epithets all dative
2. missam ... epistolam ... vestram – Abelard's *Historia Calamitatum*, in which he relates *inter alia* the story of the affair with Heloise
3. pro consolatione – Abelard supposedly wrote his *Historia* in order to console a friend by reassuring him that if he thought he was having a hard time that was nothing compared with Abelard's troubles!
4. quidam – some unknown source has delivered the letter to Heloise

5. quam ... vestram esse considerans – accusative + infinitive
   (see Appendix): 'observing that it was yours'; *ex ipsa ... tituli*
   fronte – 'from the very inscription on the front': she recognises
   his handwriting

6. tanto ... quanto – literally 'by so much ... by how much',
   with the comparatives *ardentius, carius*: 'so much the more
   eagerly ... as the more dearly'

7. amplector – 'embrace' literally and (here) metaphorically
   'cherish'

8. ut ... recreer – *ut* + subjunctive (see Appendix). She is revived
   as if by some likeness (*quadam imagine*) of him

9. cuius rem perdidi – she has lost his physical presence

10. verbis ... eius quadam imagine – she is revived by his words
    which produce an image of him

11. felle et absinthio – ablatives following *plena*, 'filled with bile
    and wormwood'

12. unice – vocative: Heloise the Abbess addresses Abelard the
    monk with a term of intimate affection

13. in te – *in* meaning here 'in respect of' or 'in the matter of';
    nisi te – 'beside yourself'

14. te pure non tua – *pure* is an adverb: 'you unconditionally not
    what was yours'

15. foedera ... dotes – 'treaties (plural of *foedus*) of marriage ...
    dowries (plural of *dos*)'; *denique* – 'in short'

16. sicut ipse nosti – *nosti* = *novisti*: 'just as you yourself knew'

17. sanctius ac validius videtur – 'seems more holy and
    wholesome'

18. amicae vocabulum ... scorti – *vocabulum*, 'the name (of)';
    amicae, 'mistress', *concubinae vel scorti*, 'concubine or whore'
    – Heloise's extraordinarily frank confession of how she saw
    their relationship

19. si non indigneris – 'if you don't take offence'; *indigneris* is
    present subjunctive

20. ut – here meaning 'so', 'in such a way'

21. quo ... humiliarem ... consequerer ... laederem – a comparative
    clause (here *amplius ... minus*) uses *quo* + subjunctive instead of
    ut: 'the more I humbled myself (from late-Latin verb *humilio*)
    ... the more gratitude (*ampliorem gratiam*) I sought in your
    eyes (*apud te*) ... the less (*minus*) I injured (*laederem*) the glory

of your pre-eminence (*excellentiae*)' – can we detect some justifiable resentment here?

22. obtulisti – perfect of *offero*: 'by that God (*per ipsum Deum*) to whom (*cui*) you have offered yourself'

23. ut ... reddas – *ut* + subjunctive (see Appendix) after *te obsecro*: 'I beg you that ...'

24. quo modo potes – *quomodo* is an adverb: 'in whatever way you can'

25. rescribendo – gerund (see Appendix): 'by writing back'

26. hoc saltem pacto – 'by this means at least'

27. ut ... vacem – *ut* + subjunctive (see Appendix); *vaco, vacare* here means 'have time for' + dative *divino obsequio*, 'divine service'

28. cum ... expeteres – *cum* + subjunctive, 'when you sought me out'

29. crebris me epistolis visitabas – he wrote to her constantly when they were lovers

30. frequenti carmine ... ponebas – a famed songwriter, Abelard's love songs for Heloise were sung throughout Paris (sadly no examples survive); *frequenti carmine* is ablative, 'with many a song'

31. me plateae ... domus resonabant – 'all the streets ... each house resounded with my name'

32. quanto ... rectius – literally, '(by) how much more properly'

33. excitares – present subjunctive: 'you should/ought to rouse me'

34. perpende ... attende – imperatives, 'consider ... heed'

35. vale unice – the affectionate address again.

2. *Francis Petrarch (1304-1374) to Cicero*

This is the first of two letters by Petrarch addressed to his literary mentor Cicero. In 1345 while he was living in Verona Petrarch had discovered in the cathedral library a collection of some 800 of Cicero's letters which had been lost for centuries. Having read them eagerly he was saddened to learn of Cicero's behaviour during the final days of the Roman Republic and following Julius Caesar's assassination. Before reading the letters, Petrarch had considered Cicero to be primarily a writer of philosophy. Now the full extent of the Roman statesman's entanglement in the dangerous politics of his times became clear to him. Better that Cicero had stayed out of politics altogether, thinks Petrarch, and devoted himself to philosophy as he often said he wished to do.

Franciscus Ciceroni suo salutem.
Epistolas tuas diu multumque perquisitas atque ubi minime rebar inventas, avidissime perlegi. Audivi multa te dicentem, multa deplorantem, multa variantem, Marce Tulli, et qui iam pridem qualis preceptor aliis fuisses noveram, nunc tandem quis tu tibi esses agnovi. Unum hoc vicissim a vera caritate profectum non iam consilium sed lamentum audi, ubicumque es, quod unus posterorum, tui nominis amantissimus, non sine lacrimis fundit.

Francis Petrarch

One of the architects of Renaissance humanism, Petrarch wrote famous love sonnets in Italian, but also a voluminous corpus of Latin works, which remained popular for centuries but are sadly now hard to find. These include his *Secretum* (a 'secret' book of imaginary dialogues expressing his personal thoughts), *De Remediis Utriusque Fortunae* ('on remedies for both good and bad fortune'), *Itinerarium* (a guide to the Holy Land) and the *Carmen Bucolicum,* a collection of pastoral poetry. In imitation of Cicero's *Epistulae ad Familiares*, Petrarch published his own Latin letters as *Rerum Familiarum Libri*. His letters written late in life were collected as *Rerum Senilium Libri*.

O inquiete semper atque anxie, vel ut verba tua recognoscas, 'o praeceps et calamitose senex', quid tibi tot contentionibus et prorsum nihil profuturis simultatibus voluisti? Ubi et aetati et professioni et fortunae tuae conveniens otium reliquisti? Quis te falsus gloriae splendor senem adolescentium bellis implicuit et per omnes iactatum casus ad indignam philosopho mortem rapuit? Heu et fraterni consilii immemor et tuorum tot salubrium praeceptorum, ceu nocturnus viator lumen in tenebris gestans, ostendisti secuturis callem, in quo ipse satis miserabiliter lapsus es.

Omitto Dionysium, omitto fratrem tuum ac nepotem, omitto, si placet, ipsum etiam Dolabellam, quos nunc laudibus ad caelum effers, nunc repentinis maledictis laceras: fuerint haec tolerabilia fortassis. Iulium quoque Caesarem praetervehor, cuius spectata clementia ipsa lacessentibus portus erat; magnum praeterea Pompeium sileo, cum quo iure quodam familiaritatis quidlibet posse videbare. Sed quis te furor in Antonium impegit? Amor credo reipublicae, quam funditus iam corruisse fatebaris. Quodsi pura fides, si libertas te trahebat, quid tibi tam familiare cum Augusto? Quid enim Bruto tuo responsurus es? 'Siquidem,' inquit, 'Octavius tibi placet, non dominum fugisse sed amiciorem dominum quaesisse videberis.'

Hoc restabat, infelix, et hoc erat extremum, Cicero, ut huic ipsi tam laudato malediceres, qui tibi non dicam malefaceret, sed malefacientibus non obstaret. Doleo vicem tuam, amice, et errorum pudet ac miseret, iamque cum eodem Bruto, 'his artibus nihil tribuo, quibus te instructissimum fuisse scio'. Nimirum quid enim iuvat alios docere, quid ornatissimis verbis semper de virtutibus loqui prodest, si te interim ipse non audias? Ah, quanto satius fuerat philosopho praesertim in tranquillo rure senuisse, 'de perpetua illa', ut ipse quodam scribis loco, 'non de hac iam exigua vita cogitantem', nullos habuisse fasces, nullis triumphis inhiasse, nullos inflasse tibi animum Catilinas. Sed haec quidem frustra. Aeternum vale, mi Cicero.

Apud superos, ad dexteram Athesis ripam, in civitate Verona Transpadanae Italiae, XVI Kalendas Quintiles, anno ab ortu Dei illius quem tu non noveras, MCCCXLV.

(Familiarum Liber 24.3)

Notes:

1. Ciceroni suo salutem – dative of the addressee (*suo* = 'dear'); the verb *dicit* with *salutem* (accusative of *salus, salutis*) is often omitted as here
2. epistolas tuas ... perquisitas ... inventas – perfect passive participles of verbs *perquiro* ('search everywhere for') and *invenio* ('find'): 'your letters which had been searched everywhere for and were found ...'
3. diu multumque – adverbs, 'long and frequently'
4. minime rebar – '(found) where least I imagined', *rebar* is imperfect of deponent verb *reor*
5. avidissime – superlative adverb
6. audivi – perfect of *audio*, here 'I learned about ...'
7. dicentem ... deplorantem ... variantem – present participles of *dico*, *deploro* and *vario*, 'while you were saying ... lamenting ... vacillating'; *multa*, 'many things'
8. Marce Tulli – vocative
9. qualis preceptor ... esses agnovi – *noveram* is pluperfect, he had already known what kind of teacher Cicero was to others

(*aliis*, dative)', now he has discovered (*agnovi*, perfect) what sort
(*quis*) he was for himself (*tibi*)

10. vicissim – adverb, 'in turn'

11. hoc ... profectum – 'this one thing having arisen (*profectum*,
from *proficiscor*) from true esteem (*vera caritate*)'

12. non iam consilium – 'no longer a counsel ...'

13. unus posterorum – 'one of your descendants', Petrarch
himself

14. amantissimus – referring to Petrarch, 'most respectful of your
name'

15. inquiete ... anxie – vocatives

16. recognoscas – present subjunctive: 'recognise your own
words'

17. praeceps et calamitose senex – vocative: not actually Cicero's
own words but adapted from the spurious *Letter to Octavian*:
'*o meam calamitosam ac praecipitem senectutem*'

18. tot contentionibus – ablative, 'by so many disputes'

19. profuturis simultatibus – 'by feuds which would gain you
(*profuturis*, future participle of *prosum*) absolutely nothing'

20. conveniens otium – 'leisure suitable for your age (*aetati*) ...'

21. quis ... falsus ... splendor – 'what sham splendour ...',
adolescentium bellis implicuit, ' ... entangled you in the wars of
the young ...', *per omnes iactatum casus* – 'driven hither and
thither through all misfortunes', *ad indignam ... mortem rapuit*,
'carried you off to an unworthy death?'

22. fraterni – *immemor* takes the genitive: Cicero took no notice of
his brother's advice nor of his own (*tuorum ... praeceptorum*)

23. ceu nocturnus viator – a simile: Cicero is like the nocturnal
traveller who holds a torch for others (*secuturis*, future participle
dative of *sequor*: 'to those who would follow') but goes astray
(*lapsus es*) himself

24. Dionysius – a freedman tutor to Cicero's son Marcus Jnr.
The people Petrarch names are those whom Cicero praises
(*laudibus*) then bemoans (*repentinis maledictis*, 'with unexpected
imprecations') in letters to his friend Atticus

25. fratrem ac nepotem – Cicero's brother Quintus and his
nephew, also called Quintus, who were both caught in the
same political snares as Cicero and who were both murdered
in the same proscriptions that claimed Cicero's life

26. Dolabella – Publius Cornelis Dolabella, Cicero's unscrupulous son-in-law, originally a supporter of Caesar who changed sides after Caesar's murder but then supported Antony

27. fuerint haec tolerabilia – 'these things might have been endurable'

28. Iulium … Caesarem … magnum Pompeium – Julius Caesar and Pompey the Great both courted Cicero's support; dismayed by Pompey's flight from Italy after Caesar had crossed the Rubicon, for a long while Cicero hesitated to take sides

29. spectata clementia – Caesar's clemency after his victory over Pompey at the battle of Pharsalus was a haven (*portus*) for his opponents (*lacessentibus*, present participle dative of *lacesso*: 'those who were attacking him'), including Cicero, who accepted with bad grace

30. cum quo iure quodam – 'with whom by some right of familiarity you seemed (*videbare*, alternative form of *videbaris*) to be able (*posse*) to do anything (*quidlibet*)'

31. in Antonium impegit – 'drove you against Antony'; Cicero's Philippic orations, delivered in 44-43 B.C., were stinging attacks on Antony and his conduct after the death of Caesar; Cicero thus earned Antony's undying hatred

32. amor credo Reipublicae – 'love of the Republic, I suppose'

33. quam … fatebaris – accusative + infinitive (see Appendix): 'you confessed that it was entirely (*funditus*) ruined'

34. quodsi … trahebat – 'even if … drew you along'

35. quid … tibi – sc. *est*: 'why did you have (to be)'

36. familiare – adverb

37. cum Augusto – Caesar's heir Octavian, later the Emperor Augustus, also sought Cicero's support against those who had killed his adoptive father, and Cicero in his turn saw the young man as a useful foil against Antony. But when Octavian and Antony formed an alliance, Cicero's hopes were dashed – the price Antony demanded for allying with the boy Caesar was Cicero's head

38. responsurus es – future participle of *respondeo*, 'what would you say in reply'

39. siquidem … Octavius tibi placet – from Cicero's *Letter to*

Brutus, I.16.7: '*si Octavius tibi placet ... non dominum fugisse, sed amiciorem dominum quaesisse videberis*', 'if Octavius pleases you ... you will seem not to have fled from a master but to have sought a more friendly master'

40. hoc restabat ... erat extremum – 'this is remaining ... this was the final deed'; *infelix* – vocative

41. ut ... malediceres – *ut* + subjunctive (see Appendix), 'that you spoke ill of' + dative *huic ipsi laudato*, 'that very man whom you had praised', i.e. Octavian

42. non dicam malefaceret – 'I will not say he was abusing you'

43. malefacientibus non obstaret – 'he was not opposing (*obstaret*, imperfect subjunctive) they who were abusing you (*malifacientibus*, present participle dative)

44. doleo vicem – 'I mourn your lot'

45. pudet ac miseret – impersonal verbs (understand *me*) followed by the genitive *errorum*

46. his artibus nihil tribuo – Letter to Brutus I.17.5 *ego vero iam iis artibus nihil tribuo, quibus Ciceronem scio instructissimum esse*, 'I now no longer set any store by those arts, in which I know that Cicero is the most skilled'

47. nimirum – 'to be sure'

48. prodest – takes the dative, 'what benefit to speak (*loqui*) about virtues (*virtutibus*)'

49. audias – present subjunctive, 'if you would not listen to yourself'

50. quanto satius – 'how much more preferable'; *senuisse* – 'to have grown old'

51. quodam ... loco – *Letter to Atticus*, X.8.8: '*tempus est nos de illa perpetua iam, non de hac exigua vita cogitare*', 'it is time that we now think about that perpetual life, not about this brief life'

52. nullos habuisse fasces – accusative + infinitive; the *fasces* were the symbols of consular power (English, 'fascist')

53. inhiasse – 'that you had coveted no triumphs'

54. inflasse ... Catilinas – 'that no Catilines had puffed up your ego'; Catiline was the conspirator whom Cicero exposed during his consulship in 63 B.C.

55. apud superos – 'among the living'

56. Athesis – the river Adige in Verona

57. Quintiles – the original name for the fifth month (not changed

to July until after Cicero's death), see *Annus Horribilis*, Ch. 5

58. ortu – perfect participle of *orior* here = 'birth'; *quem non noveras* – 'whom you did not know'.

3. *Desiderius Erasmus (c.1466/9–1536) to Doctor Francis*

In this extract from a letter written in 1518 to Dr John Francis – physician to Cardinal Wolsey – Erasmus complains about the state of English houses and hygiene.

Erasmus Roterodamus Francisco Cardinalis Eboracensis Medico S.

Frequenter et admirari et dolere soleo, qui fiat ut Britannia tot iam annis assidua pestilentia vexetur, praesertim sudore letali, quod malum paene videtur habere peculiare. Legimus civitatem a diutina pestilentia liberatam, consilio philosophi mutatis aedificiis. Aut me fallit animus, aut simili ratione liberari possit Anglia.

Primum quam coeli partem spectent fenestrae ostiave nihil habent pensi: deinde sic fere constructa sunt conclavia, ut nequaquam sint perflabilia, quod inprimis admonet Galenus. Tum magnam parietis partem habent vitreis tessellis pellucidam, quae sic admittunt lumen ut ventos excludant, et tamen per rimulas admittunt auram illam colatam, aliquanto pestilentiorem, ibi diu quiescentem. Tum sola fere strata sunt argilla, tum scirpis palustribus, qui subinde sic renovantur, ut fundamentum maneat aliquoties annos viginti, sub se fovens sputa, vomitus, proiectam cervisiam et piscium reliquias, aliasque sordes non nominandas. Hinc mutato coelo vapor quidam exhalatur, mea sententia minime salubris humano corpori ... Bene uale, uir humanissime; cui debeo plurimum.

Notes:

1. Francisco ... Medico – dative of the addressee; *Cardinalis Eboracensis* – genitive, 'of the Archbishop of York'; S. – for *salutem* (*dicit*), the traditional formula

2. et ... et – 'both ... and'; both infinitives *admirari* (deponent not passive) and *dolere* after *soleo*, 'I am accustomed to ...'

3. qui fiat – 'how it can happen ...', *fiat* is subjunctive of *fio* (cf. *fiat lux*) followed by *ut* + passive subjunctive *vexetur*, '... that Britain is troubled by ...', *assidua pestilentia* – ablative

4. praesertim – adverb, 'especially'; *sudore letali* – 'by the lethal sweat'

5. videtur habere peculiare – 'seems to have peculiarly (i.e. uniquely)'

6. legimus – as customary in Latin prose writers, the 'royal' we

7. civitatem ... liberatam – sc. *esse*: accusative + infinitive, 'that a city had been freed ...'; *duitina pestilentia* – ablative, 'from a long-lasting plague'

8. consilio ... mutatis aedificiis – *mutatis* is the perfect participle passive of *muto*, 'change'; literally: 'by a plan with the buildings having been altered', so 'for modifying the buildings'

9. me fallit animus – 'my understanding deceives me'

10. simili ratione – 'by a similar method'

11. fenestrae ostiave – 'the windows or doors', subjects of subjunctive *spectent*

12. nihil habent pensi – literally: 'they have nothing of thought (partitive genitive of *pensum*)' = 'they care nothing about'

13. fere – adverb, 'almost' or 'generally'

14. conclavia – 'rooms'; *nequaquam* – 'by no means'; *perflabilia* – 'ventilated'

15. inprimis – usually *imprimis*, 'especially'; Galen was a physician of the second century A.D. whose writings remained standard medical textbooks in the middle ages

16. parietis – genitive, 'of the wall'; *pellucidam* – 'transparent'; *vitreis tessellis* – ablative, 'with glass panes'

17. sic ... ut – 'in this way ... as ...'

18. et tamen – 'in spite of which'

19. per rimulas – 'through small cracks'

20. auram ... colatam – *colatam* is the perfect passive participle of *colare*, 'strain, filter', so 'air which has been filtered'

21. aliquanto pestilentiorem – 'sometimes more unhealthy'

22. quiescentem – present participle of *quiesco*: 'stagnating'

23. tum sola ... tum scirpis – 'sometimes ... at other times (*tum ... tum*) the floors (*sola*) are covered (*strata sunt*) with clay (*argilla*), with rushes from the marshes (*scirpis palustribus*)

24. subinde – adverb, 'from time to time'; *renovantur* – passive, 'are refreshed'

25. ut ... maneat – *ut* + subjunctive (see Appendix); *fundamentum* – 'foundation' or 'floor'

26. aliquoties annos viginti – accusative of duration of time, 'sometimes for twenty years'

27. se fovens – 'keeping itself warm'; *fovens* is the present participle of *foveo*

28. sub ... sputa, vomitus ... reliquias – *sub* + accusative plurals of *sputum* (neuter), *vomitus* (fourth declension), *reliquiae* ('leftovers', 'remains')

29. proiectam cervisiam – *proiectam* from *proicio*, 'throw away' so literally: 'beer which had been thrown away' i.e. 'spilt beer' (cf. Spanish *cerveza*)

30. aliasque sordes non nominandas – 'other filth not to be named'; *nominandas* is the gerundive (see Appendix), sc. *esse*: 'that must not be named'

31. mutato coelo – ablative, 'with a change in the weather'; *vapor ... exhalatur*, 'a vapour is given off'

32. mea sententia – 'in my opinion'

33. minime salubris – 'the least conducive to health'; *humano corpori* – dative.

4. *Richard Bentley (1662–1742) to Graevius*

One of the great classical scholars of his day, Bentley was a master of textual criticism and used his skill to expose several supposed ancient works as later forgeries, famously the *Epistles of Phalaris* which had been published by Charles Boyle in 1695. Disputatious by nature, he also engaged in the debate between 'ancients' and 'moderns' satirized by Swift in his *Battle of the Books* (1704). Bentley never left England, nor was he fluent in modern European languages, but he nonetheless carried on correspondence with a variety of European scholars – in Latin, naturally.

'When men of learning have ceased to possess a common Language, they will soon forget that they have a common Country; they will no longer regard each other as intellectual compatriots; they will be Englishmen, Frenchmen, Dutchmen, but not Scholars.' (Preface to *The Correspondence of Richard Bentley*, 1842)

Viro Maximo J. G. Graevio S. P.D. Richardus Bentleius.

Doleo equidem, et iamdudum vix mihi ignosco, quod literis tuis, quae abhinc mensibus amplius quinque ad me perlata sunt, non maturius rescripserim. Sed dabis, uti spero, hanc veniam homini et infinitis negotiis occupato, et ex illo ferme tempore procul ab Urbe et Literatorum consuetudine absenti.

Nuper vero admodum Londinum reversus, ubi fixum larem habiturus esse videor in posterum, cum nihil prius in animo haberem, quam ut prima occasione gratias tibi per epistolam cum meo tum aliorum nomine quam maximas agerem pro nobilissima illa et divina Oratione, qua incomparabilis Reginae memoriam Aeternitati consecrasti: ecce tibi, peropportune se mihi offert, qui tibi has tradet Grodeckius, in Bataviam vestram contendans. Scias itaque me Exempla illa ex tua sententia Episcopis Salisburiensi, Lichfieldensi, et qui tecum communicavit Ciceronis Philosophica, Norwicensi, tradita curavisse: minime autem Doctori Smith, homini alioqui probo et erudito; verum quod tu, opinor, haud inaudiveras, animo erga Regem Gulielmum et Beatae MARIAE memoriam non parum iniquo. Visum est igitur, exemplum Smithio destinatum Archiepiscopo Cantuariensi dare; et alterum, quod mihi proprium consignasti, Archiepiscopo Eboracensi; ne summorum Praesulum, nec minus eruditione quam dignitate praecellentium vel ignarus vel immemor fuisse viderere. Qui omnes cum ob hanc Orationem tum ob infinita alia praeclari ingenii monumenta, quae per omnium ora manusque volitant, omniumque oculos in te convertunt, se plurimum te amare et colere prolixe significarunt ... Vale, vir celeberrime, et me ama. Londini, III. Kal. Dec. MDCXCV.

Notes:

1. Viro Maximo J.G. Graevio – dative of the addressee; Johann Georg Graevius (1632-1703) of the University of Utrecht, was an internationally renowned German classicist who had close links with William III and Queen Mary; though he and Bentley never met, they carried on a long and friendly correspondence

2. S.P.D. – *salutem plurimam dicit*, the customary address, literally, 'says greatest greetings' or 'says many a greeting'

3. iamdudum – 'after all this time'

4. mihi ignosco – *ignosco* puts the object in the dative, so 'forgive myself'

5. quod ... rescripserim – 'that I have not replied' (*scripserim,*

perfect subjunctive), a similar construction to the *ut* + subjunctive

6. abhinc mensibus amplius quinque – after a comparative the ablative can express 'than …'; *quinque* is indeclinable: 'more than five months ago'

7. perlata sunt – perfect passive of *perfero*

8. maturius – comparative adverb, 'sooner'

9. dabis … hanc veniam – *veniam dare* means 'to grant a favour'

10. uti – variant spelling of *ut*, with indicative = 'as'

11. homini … occupato … absenti – datives following *dabis hanc veniam*

12. ab Urbe – Bentley means from Cambridge, his university

13. Literatorum consuetudine – 'from the company of literary men'; a *Litterator* is an elementary school teacher, but presumably here = *litteratus*

14. Londinum reversus – *reversus* is active, from deponent *revertor*; names of cities don't require the preposition *ad*

15. fixum larem – *fixum* is the perfect participle of *figo*; a *Lar* is the Roman household god, so metaphorically a home: 'a permanent residence'

16. habiturus esse videor – where English prefers the impersonal construction 'it seems that …', Latin likes to use the passive of *video* as a personal verb, so here *videor*, literally: 'I seem to be about to have …', i.e. 'it seems that I will own …'

17. in animo haberem – literally, 'I have in mind', i.e. 'I intend' or 'I am resolved to'; *quam* – 'than …', English wants an infinitive here but Latin uses *ut* + subjunctive

18. ut … gratias tibi agerem – *ut* + subjunctive (see Appendix): 'to thank you'; *prima occasione* – ablative of time, 'at the first opportunity'

19. gratias … quam maximas – *quam* + superlative = 'as x as possible'

20. Oratione – a eulogy on Queen Mary, who had recently died (28th December, 1694); *aeternitati* – dative

21. ecce tibi – as Graevius reads this, the deliverer of Bentley's letter will be standing in front of him

22. peropportune – adverb

23. tradet Grodeckius … contendans – he will deliver the letter

(*has*, i.e. the *litteras*) since he is travelling to Batavia

24. scias ... me ... curavisse – accusative + perfect infinitive (see Appendix)

25. exempla illa ... tradita – copies of the Oration sent to Bentley by Graevius to be delivered to the Bishops

26. ex tua sententia – Graevius had specified the recipients in a previous letter

27. Episcopis – dative: 'to the Bishops', Lloyd (Lichfield), Burnet (Salisbury) and Moore (Norwich)

28. Philosophica – post-Classical adjective *philosophicus* (= Classical *philosophia*), here neuter plural accusative after verb *communico*, 'discuss'

29. minime autem Doctori Smith – 'but not to Dr Smith', whom Graevius had mentioned should receive a copy; Bentley then explains why

30. homini alioqui probo et erudito – 'in other respects a virtuous and learned man', all dative agreeing with *Doctori*

31. inaudiveras – pluperfect

32. animo erga ... parum iniquo – literally 'in his heart not a little unfavourable towards', so 'unfavourably inclined towards'

33. visum est – 'it seemed (better)'

34. exemplum ... destinatum – the copy destined for Smith

35. quod mihi proprium consignasti – the copy Graevius had given to Bentley

36. ne ... fuisse viderere – negative of *ut* + subjunctive (see Appendix); *viderere* = *videreris*, imperfect passive subjunctive: 'lest you seem to have been ...'

37. ignarus vel immemor – both followed by genitives, hence *summorum Praesulum ... praecellentium*; a *Praesul* in medieval Latin is a prelate

38. cum ... tum – 'both ... and'

39. praeclari ingenii – genitive after *infinita alia monumenta*

40. volitant – 'travel to and fro'

41. se ... amare et colere significarunt – accusative + infinitive (see Appendix)

42. Londini, III. Kal. Dec. – locative 'at London'; for Roman dates see *Annus Horribilis*, Ch. 5.

5. *Tobias Smollett (1721–1771) to Doctor Fizes*

Sterne on Smollett 'Smelfungus'

'The learned Smelfungus travelled from Boulogne to Paris, from Paris to Rome, and so on; but he set out with the spleen and jaundice, and every object he pass'd by was discoloured or distorted. He wrote an account of them, but 'twas nothing but the account of his miserable feelings.' (*A Sentimental Journey Through France and Italy*, 1768)

In 1763, author and valetudinarian Tobias Smollett undertook a journey to southern Europe in the hope of finding a climate more conducive to his frail state of health. But by the time he reached Montpelier in the south of France Smollett had begun to suffer again with his 'asthmatical disorder' following continual rain which also brought on 'fever, cough, spitting and lowness of spirits'. In desperation he wrote to a renowned local physician, Dr Fizes, whom Smollett in his typically dyspeptic manner thought was probably a quack: 'Notwithstanding his great age and great wealth, he will still scramble up two pair of stairs for a fee of six livres; and without a fee, he will give his advice to no person whatsoever. He is said to have great practice in the venereal branch, and to be frequented by persons of both sexes infected with this distemper.'

This letter was included by Smollett in his book *Travels Through France and Italy (1766)*. For Smollett, himself a medical man, the correct language in which to communicate with a fellow physician was Latin. But the French doctor responded in French:

> 'I thought it a little extraordinary that a learned professor should reply in his mother tongue to a case put in Latin … I was obliged to conclude either that he did not understand Latin, or that he had not taken the trouble to read my memoire.'

In fact, though Smollett did not want to admit it, his French colleague seems to have correctly diagnosed tuberculosis (consumption). Astonishingly, neither party ever met nor was any physical examination thought necessary!

Annum aetatis post quadragesimum tertium. Temperamentum humidum, crassum, pituitâ repletum, catarrhis saepissimè profligatum. Catarrhus, febre, anxietate et dyspnoea, nunquam non comitatus. Irritatio membrane pituitariae trachaealis, *tussim initio aridam, siliquosam, deinde vero excretionem copiosam excitat: sputum albumini ovi simillimum* …

Quibusdam adhinc annis, exercitationibus juvenilibus subito remissis, in vitam sedentariam lapsum. Animo in studia severiora converso, fibrae gradatim laxabantur. Inter legendum et scribendum inclinato corpore in pectus malum ruebat. Morbo ingruenti affectio scorbutica auxilium tulit. Invasio prima nimium aspernata. Venientibus hostibus non occursum. Cunctando res non restituta. Remedia convenientia stomachus perhorrescebat. Gravescente dyspnoea phlebotomia frustra tenata. Sanguinis missione vis vitae diminuta. Fiebat pulsus debilior, respiratio difficilior. In peius ruunt omnia. Febris anomala in febriculum continuam mutata. Dyspnoea confirmata. Fibrarum compages soluta. Valetudo penitus eversa …

Hieme pluviosâ regnante dolores renovantur; tametsi tempore sereno equitatio profuit. Aestate morbus vix ullum progrediebatur. Autumno, valetudine plus declinatâ, thermis Bathoniensibus solatium haud frustra quaesitum. Aqua ista mirè medicata, externè aeque ac internè adhibita, malis levamen attulit. Hiems altera, frigida, horrida, diuturna, innocua tamen successit. Vere novo casus atrox diras procellas animo inmisit; toto corpore, totâ mente tumultuatur. Patriâ relictâ, tristitiâ, solicitudo, indignatio, et sevissima recordatio sequuntur. Inimici priores furore inveterato revertuntur. Rediit febris hectica; rediit asthma cum anxietate, tussi, et dolore lateris lancinante.

(*Letter the Eleventh*, Montpelier Nov. 12 1763)

Notes:

1. the letter opens by describing (at great length) Smollett's symptoms: he writes in the third person throughout. Begin with 'The patient is …'

2. temperamentum – his constitution; *pituitâ repletum* – the accent above the final 'a' of *pituitâ* indicates it is ablative, following *repletum* (participle of *repleo*) agreeing with *temperamentum*: 'overflowing with phlegm'

3. comitatus – 'accompanied (by)' hence ablatives *febre*, *anxietate* et *dyspnoea* ('shortness of breath')

4. trachaealis – genitive, an adjective derived from *trachea*, a

late-Latinisation of the Greek word for windpipe

5. simillimum – superlative adjective, followed by dative *albumini* and genitive *ovi*: 'very like the white of an egg'. The detailed description of symptoms continues long after this

6. quibusdam … annis – *quibusdam* is ablative plural from *quidam*, agreeing with *annis*: Latin regularly puts the 'time when' in the ablative case

7. exercitationibus juvenilibus … remissis – ablative absolute (see Appendix), 'after youthful activities had been abandoned'

8. lapsum – perfect participle from deponent *labor* used impersonally (sc. *est*), literally 'there was a sinking into'

9. animo … converso – ablative absolute, 'having turned his mind'; *in studio serveriora* – 'toward more laborious studies'

10. laxabantur – passive, 'were relaxed'

11. legendum et scribendum – gerunds (see Appendix)

12. inclinato corpore – another ablative absolute

13. morbo ingruenti – dative after *auxilium tulit*, literally 'brought help to the violently attacking malady'

14. scorbutica – adjective derived from the Neo-Latin word *scorbutus*, 'scurvy', in agreement with *affectio*

15. invasio – a post-Classical word (English 'invasion') for the Classical *incursio*

16. aspernata – perfect participle from deponent *aspernor*, 'scorn/spurn'; *nimium* – 'unduly'

17. occursum – participle from *occurro* used impersonally, literally 'there was not a counterattack': translate 'he did not take measures against …'; *venientibus hostibus* – 'the returning enemy', dative following *occursum*

18. cunctando – another gerund, ablative, 'by delaying'

19. gravescente dyspnoea – ablative, 'with the shortness of breath worsening'

20. phlebotomia – a phlebotomy, i.e. blood-letting; *tenata* – perfect participle from *tempto*, 'having been tried'

21. diminuta – perfect participle from verb *deminuo* (English 'diminish')

22. fiebat – imperfect of *fio*; *debilior* … *difficilior* – comparative adjectives

23. in peius – 'into a worse state'

24. febris anomola – 'irregular fever'; *febriculum* – diminutive; *mutata* – perfect passive participle with *febris*, 'the fever was changed …'

25. fibrarum compages – 'the binding of the fibres'; *soluta* – perfect passive participle from *solvo*, 'loosen'

26. penitus – adverb, 'entirely'

27. hieme pluviosa regnante – ablative absolute (see Appendix), 'while rainy winter was holding sway'

28. tempore sereno – 'in clear weather'

29. profuit – understand *sibi* after *prosum*: 'riding was of benefit to him'

30. valetudine plus declinata – another ablative absolute, 'having declined more'

31. Bathoniensibus – locative, with *thermis*, of adjective *Bathoniensis*: he sought (*quaesitum*) the solace (*solatium*) of the Bath waters

32. mirè – adverb, 'wonderfully'

33. aeque – 'alike', 'equally'

34. malis levamen – 'relief from evils'

35. hiems altera – the following winter, though long-lasting (*diuturna*) proved harmless (*innocua*)

36. vere novo – the next spring

37. casus atrox – the death of his daughter Elizabeth, aged 15 or 16; *diras procellas* – 'dreadful disturbances'

38. tumultuatur – passive, 'he was agitated, disturbed'

39. patria relicta tristitia – another ablative absolute, 'having left home in sadness'

40. sevissima – for *saevissima*, with *recordatio*, 'the most cruel recollection'

41. inimici priores – 'his previous enemies returned (*revertuntur*, from deponent *revertor*) with *inveterato* (*inveteratus*, 'firmly rooted', 'established') fury'

42. febris … hectica – 'hectic fever', defined by Webster's medical dictionary as 'a fever of irritation and debility, occurring usually at an advanced stage of exhausting disease, as in pulmonary consumption'

43. lancinante – ablative of present participle from verb *lancino*, 'tear', so 'a tearing pain in his side'.

6. Laurence Sterne (1713–1768) to John Hall-Stevenson

The author of Tristram Shandy was of a rather different temperament to Smollett. He is not known for his Latin, but rather as one of the most daring writers of English. Fittingly, then, this Latin letter – the only one in Sterne's published correspondence – plays as fast and loose with the language of Cicero as Sterne was wont to do with his own native tongue. Dashed off in the midst of a crowded, noisy coffee-house, he hardly had the leisure to consult his grammar books, dictionaries or Classical exemplars anyway. Nor, being Sterne, would he have thought such gramamtical niceties anything other than finnicky pedantry. John Hall-Stevenson, a distant cousin, was a lifelong friend as well as a notorious rake. Soon after writing this letter, Stevenson and Sterne were in London together supervising the publication of Sentimental Journey. Sterne died in March 1768.

> ### Sterne in amore
>
> In 1758 Sterne's wife Elizabeth suffered a breakdown after discovering her husband's affair with a maidservant. In 1766, she decided to remain in France when he travelled back to England. Sterne then met Mrs Elizabeth Draper and promptly fell in love – they exchanged many frank letters – though she was married and her husband, who was stationed in Bombay, soon summoned her back to India. 'Eliza' was only one of Sterne's amorous admirers: many revealing letters from other ladies of quality were discovered after his death and burnt by one of his friends.

Literas vestras lepidissimas, mi consobrine, consobrinis meis omnibus carior, accepi die Veneris; sed posta non rediebat versus Aquilonem eo die, aliter scripsissem prout desiderabas. Nescio quid est materia cum me, sed sum fatigatus et aegrotus de meâ uxore plus quam unquam – et sum possessus cum diabolo qui pellet me in urbem – et tu es possessus cum eodem malo spiritu qui te tenet in deserto esse tentatum ancillis tuis, et perturbatum uxore tuâ – crede mihi, mi Antoni, quod isthaec non est via ad salutem sive hodiernam; sive eternam; num tu incipis cogitare de pecuniâ, quae, ut ait Sanctus Paulus, est radix omnium malorum, et non satis dicis in corde tuo, ego Antonius de Castello Infirmo, sum jam quadraginta et plus annos natus, et explevi octavum meum lustrum, et tempus est me curare, et meipsum Antonium facere hominem felicem et liberum, et mihimet

*ipsi benefacere, ut exhortatur Solomon, qui dicit quod nihil est melius in hâc
vitâ quàm quòd homo vivat festivè et quòd edat et bibat, et bono fruatur quia
hoc est sua portio et dos in hoc mundo.*

*Nunc te scire vellemus, quòd non debeo esse reprehendi pro festinando eundo
ad Londinum, quia Deus est testis, quòd non propero prae gloria, et pro me
ostendere; nam diabolus iste qui me intravit, non est diabolus vanus, aut
consobrinus suus Lucifer − sed est diabolus amabundus, qui non vult sinere
me esse solum; nam cùm non cumbenbo cum uxore meâ, sum mentulatior
quàm par est − et sum mortaliter in amore − et sum fatuus; ergo tu me, mi
care Antoni, excusabis, quoniam tu fuisti in amore, et per mare et per terras
ivisti et festinâsti sicut diabolus eodem te propellente diabolo. Habeo multa ad
te scribere − sed scribo hanc epistolam in domo coffeatariâ et plenâ sociorum
strepitosorum, qui non permittent me cogitare unam cogitationem.*

*Saluta amicum Panty meum, cujus literis respondebo − saluta amicos in
domo Gisbrosensi, et oro, credas me vinculo consobrinitatis et amoris ad te, mi
Antoni, devinctissimum.*

(To J- H- S-, Esq., December 1767)

Notes:

1. litteras vestras − 'your letter'; Latin uses the plural where
   English prefers the singular. The letter to which he is replying
   was presumably also in Latin
2. lepidissimas − a superlative, *lepidus* being a good Classical word
   for 'charming', 'witty'
3. mi consobrine − vocative, *consobrinus* is strictly speaking
   a maternal cousin, while a paternal cousin would be a
   patruelis
4. carior − comparative of adjective *carus*, 'dear', with the ablative
   consobrinis meis omnibus: 'dearer than all my cousins'
5. accepi − perfect tense of *accipio*
6. die Veneris − ablative of *dies*, genitive of *Venus*: 'on the day of
   Venus', i.e. Friday, cf. French *vendredi*, Italian *venerdi*
7. posta − not Latin, possibly borrowed from Italian
8. rediebat − imperfect of *redeo*
9. versus Aquilonem − preposition 'towards' + accusative of
   aquilo, capitalised so 'The North'
10. eo die − ablative of time, 'on that day'

11. scripsissem – pluperfect subjunctive, 'I would have written'

12. prout – 'just as'

13. desiderabas – imperfect of *desidero*: my copy of Sterne's correspondence prints *desideradas*, which is presumably a mistake

14. materia – a nice bit of Anglo-Latin! *Materia* is 'matter' as in 'stuff', 'material'; but Sterne employs it with the colloquial English meaning: 'I don't know what's the matter with me'

15. meâ – note the accent on the 'a' indicating a long vowel, so this word is in the ablative case (as it should be following preposition *de*)

16. plus quam – 'more than'

17. diabolo – ablative of *diabolus*, unsurprisingly a Church Latin word; *eodem malo spiritu* – also ablative after *cum*: 'with that same evil spirit', Sterne's euphemism for lust?

18. in deserto esse tentatum – cf. *Luke* 4.1: '*et (Jesus) agebatur a Spiritu in desertum … et tentabatur a diabolo*', 'and he was led by the Spirit into the wilderness … and was tempted by the devil'

19. mi Antoni – vocative, perhaps jokingly Stevenson is Antony to Sterne's Caesar?

20. isthaec – feminine form of pronoun *istic*, 'that (*via*) of yours'

21. salutem – Classical 'health, safety', biblical 'salvation'

22. radix omnium malorum – 1 *Timothy* 6.10, 'for the love of money (*cupiditas*) is the root of all evils'

23. de Castello Infirmo – Skelton Castle, Stevenson's home, also known as 'Crazy Castle', demolished at the end of the eighteenth century; *infirmum*, 'weak, feeble', so 'crazy' in the sense of rambling and ramshackle

24. quadraginta et plus annos natus – literally: 'forty and more years born'

25. octavum … lustrum – a *lustrum* being a period of five years

26. meipsum – *me* + *ipsum*, 'me myself'

27. mihimet – suffix -*met* for emphasis: 'to me myself', made even more emphatic with addition of *ipsi*

28. Solomon – *Ecclesiastes* 2.24: *Nonne melius est comedere et bibere, et ostendere animae suae bona de laboribus suis?*, 'There is nothing better for man than that he should eat and drink and that he should make his soul enjoy good in his labour'

29. vellemus – imperfect subjunctive of *volo*, the plural (the 'royal' we)

is common in Latin writing: 'We would wish you to know'

30. quod non debeo esse — Sterne uses *quod* to introduce a 'that
    …' clause where Classical Latin would use the accusative +
    infinitive construction

31. pro festinando eundo — gerunds of *festino, festinare* and *eo, ire*:
    'for going in a hurry'

32. prae gloria — 'on account of glory'

33. pro me ostendere — 'for making an exhibition of myself'

34. consobrinus suus Lucifer — the Devil himself, the 'cousin' of
    the other devil already referred to

35. amabundus — another non-Classical word, the suffix –*bundus*
    means 'abounding in' as in *floribundus*

36. cumbenbo — possibly he meant to write *cumbendo*, the
    ablative gerund of *cumbo, cumbere*, a medieval Latin substitute
    for the Classical *cubo, cubare*. The stem -*cumbo* survives in the
    compounds like *accumbo* and *recumbo* (English 'recumbent').
    Just as English 'go to bed' has a different meaning when we say
    'go to bed with someone', so *cubo/cumbo* followed by *cum*

37. mentulatior — a comparative from *mentulatus*, 'having a penis'
    — suggests a pun: 'more cock-y than is proper'. Since Sterne's
    wife is absent, he is feeling randy and so hurries off to London
    to satisfy his urges — but claims that because he is in love he
    does not deserve censure

38. festinasti sicut diabolus — you hurried to the same place (*eodem*)
    just like a devil with a devil urging you on (*te propellente
    diabolo*)

39. domo coffeataria — coffee-house

40. saluta — imperative: 'send greetings'

41. Gisbrosensi — Guisborough in N. Yorks. Sterne's home was
    Shandy Hall in Coxwold, between Guisborough and York

42. credas — subjunctive but with force of imperative, sc. *esse* with
    me … devinctissium to make accusative + infinitive: 'I ask that you
    believe I am most devoted to you (*ad te*)'

43. vinculo consobrinitatis — 'in the bond of cousinship'

44. J- H- S - Sterne's letters were published posthumously by his
    daughter in 1775. She obliterated the names of many of his
    correspondents

45. I am grateful to Dr David Noy for his helpful correspondence
    about this letter.

Recommended Reading:

Abelard and Heloise   *The Letters*
                             Penguin Classics

Betty Radice's classic English translation of the correspondence.

Richard Bentley   *The Correspondence*
                             George Olms

Bentley's complete correspondence, both English and Latin (originally published in 1842 in two volumes).

Erasmus (ed. Facer)   *Erasmus and His Times*
                             Bolchazy-Carducci

A reprint of G.S. Facer's selection (originally published in 1951) mostly from Erasmus' letters, with helpful translation notes and vocabulary.

Petrarch (ed. Kallendorg) *Selected Letters*
                             Bryn Mawr Commentaries

A slim, ring-bound edition of selections with grammatical notes for the student.

Tobias Smollett   *Travels Through France and Italy*
                             Oxford World's Classics

Laurence Sterne   *The Letters of Laurence Sterne*
                             Kessinger Publishing

CHAPTER 6

NEO-LATIN PROSE

The tag 'Neo-Latin' might lead you to imagine some new-fangled development in the language, some radical change adopted by zealous reformers. Not at all. Neo-Latin (or Renaissance Latin as it is sometimes known) is nothing more than Classical Latin revived, albeit written by people for whom Latin was not their mother tongue. It differs only from Cicero's usage in employing by necessity a somewhat expanded vocabulary, especially when new developments in science or discoveries in lands unknown to the ancients are being discussed. The term Neo-Latin, then, is simply a way of distinguishing these works from their Biblical and Medieval predecessors.

The Neo-Latinists produced a vast and original corpus of Latin literature. These days, though, most students of Latin tend to confine themselves to reading ancient Roman authors. But without the efforts of the Neo-Latinists in rediscovering and disseminating those texts we would now have little more surviving from antiquity than a handful of Cicero's philosophical works and Virgil's *Aeneid*. Despite their current neglect, Renaissance and post-Renaissance Latin works played a vital role in spreading the new secular learning across a Europe-wide community of scholars for whom Latin was the lingua franca of ideas.

Some of the most important books of the modern age – not just literature but scientific treatises, philosophical and political works – were written in Latin. Take, for example, the *Novum Organum* (1620) of Francis Bacon (1561-1621), in which he expounded an inductive

---

Neo-Latin on the web

Relatively few Neo-Latin texts are currently available in print. Fortunately, there are websites where many of these works can be found, including:

The Philological Museum Library of Humanistic Texts: http://www.philological.bham.ac.uk/

The Latin Library: http://www.thelatinlibrary.com/neo.html

logic based on empirical observation that laid the foundations of the modern scientific method; and the *Philosophiae Naturalis Principia Mathematica* (1687) of Sir Isaac Newton (1642-1727), wherein are explained his laws of motion and gravitation.

All rather highbrow, it's true, but Neo-Latin has other hidden charms: poetry, plays and chatty letters (for the latter see Chapter 5) were also produced in abundance. As late as the 1770s, Dr Johnson was appreciated for his skill in extemporising Latin verses in correct Classical metres (see Chapter 7).

A MISCELLANY OF NEO-LATIN PROSE

Below you will find a tiny selection from an almost wholly neglected genre. In one brief chapter I could not hope to provide a representative picture of Neo-Latin, but have chosen extracts purely for their intrinsic interest and 'readability'. Two important contributors to this category of writing – *viz.* Petrarch and Erasmus – can be found in Chapters 5 and 7.

1. *Peter Martyr of Angleria (1457-1526)*

Peter Martyr was an Italian contemporary of Columbus whose favoured position at the Spanish court gave him access to first-hand accounts of Columbus' voyages. Martyr's history of near-contemporary events, *De Orbe Novo*, unfolded in a series of accounts which he called 'decades', because each is divided into ten chapters. Like Erasmus, Martyr regarded Latin as a living, vernacular language in which modern ideas could be given expression; he was not concerned whether his writing was suitably Ciceronian or not. His style is vividly colloquial – some of the decades purport to be letters – and he freely introduces new words adopted from the natives of the New World: *canoa* ('canoe'), *canibal* ('cannibal'), *carib* (another name for cannibal, whence 'Caribbean'), *iucca* ('yucca') and *Taino* (the native peoples themselves) being a few examples. Instead of the pejorative Classical word *barbari*, Martyr prefers the neutral *incola* ('inhabitants') or *indigena* ('natives', whence 'indigenous'). His independent stance, often highly critical of the Spanish conquistadors, makes him a truly modern historian. And his racy narrative makes for compelling reading.

A GRUESOME SOUPÇON

In the year 1509 the conquistador Diego de Nicuesa and his crew have
been shipwrecked off the coast of what is now Panama ...

Oppressit socios eius [Nicuesa's] *egestas tanta, ut neque a scabiosis canibus,
quos venatus et tutelae causa secum habebant, in certaminibus nanque cum nudis
incolis canum opera plurimum utebantur, neque aliquando a peremptis incolis
abstinuerunt. Non enim ibi fructificantes arbores aut volucres quas Dariennem
alere diximus procreari, ac proinde terram minime frequentem habitatoribus
reperiebant. Convenerunt e sociis quidam de cane macerrimo emendo, qui iam
fere et ipse deficiebat ob esuriem, multos praebent canis domino auri pesos, id
est aureos castellanos. Canem excoriant comedendum. Scabiosam canis pellem
capitis ossibus appensis inter dumeta proxima proiecerunt. Postridie pedes
quidam e sociis in abiectam pellam incidit vermibus iam refertam ac semifetente,
domum asportavit. Excussis vermibus pellem in ollam coquendam coniecit,
coctam edit. Adcoctae pellis ius cum suis multi paropsidibus singulos castellanos
aureos pro singulis iuris paropsidibus offerentes accurrebant.*

Notes:

1. I am grateful to Professor Geoffrey Eatough of Lampeter
   University for providing me with his (as yet unpublished)
   edition of Martyr's second *Decade*, from which this extract
   is taken. See the recommended reading below for details of
   Eatough's comprehensive edition of the first *Decade*

2. egestas tanta – 'such great want', i.e. hunger: Nicuesa's crew
   (*socios eius*) were starving

3. ut ... abstinuerunt – either as a result clause, 'so that they
   abstained from ...', (in which case the verb should be
   subjunctive *abstinuerint*) or perhaps here *ut* = 'to such an
   extent that ...'

4. neque ... neque – 'neither ... nor'. This first sentence has
   several subordinate clauses, but the main clause is *ut neque a
   scabiosis canibus neque a peremptis incolis abstinuerunt*

5. a scabiosis canibus ... a peremptis incolis – ablatives after
   abstinuerunt, 'from mangy dogs ... from slaughtered natives';
   peremptus is the perfect participle passive of *perimo*, 'kill, destroy'

6. quos venatus et tutelae causa – postposition *causa* + genitive
   = 'for the sake of'; the dogs that they had with them (*secum*

habebant) for hunting (*venatus* is fouth declension, genitive
−*us*) and as guard dogs (*tutela*)

7. nanque − sc. *namque*

8. certaminibus cum nudis incolis − 'in battles with the naked
   natives', Martyr often stresses the nudity of the natives in
   contrast to the heavily armoured Spanish

9. utebantur − *utor* is deponent (not passive) followed by the
   ablative *opera*: 'they (the Spaniards) made much (adverb
   plurimum) use of dogs (genitive plural *canum*) in this work'

10. fructificantes arbores ... procreari − 'neither fruit trees nor
    birds were bred'; *non ... aut* is better in English as 'neither ...
    nor'

11. quas Dariennem alere diximus − accusative + infinitive (see
    Appendix) following *diximus* (Martyr has mentioned the same
    point earlier): 'which we have said that Darien supports', i.e.
    in the region around the colony of Darien

12. proinde ... reperiebant − for this reason (i.e. the lack of food),
    they found the land empty of inhabitants; *minime* here =
    'not'

13. convenerunt − subject is *e sociis quidam*, 'some men from the
    company'

14. de cane macerrimo emendo − *emendo* is gerundive (see
    Appendix), ablative following preposition *de* and agreeing
    with *cane macerrimo*, literally: 'concerning an exceedingly thin
    dog to-be-purchased'

15. et ipse deficiebat ob esuriem − the poor dog himself was
    almost dead from starvation!

16. aureos castellanos − gold pieces, *castellani* (from Castille);
    domino − dative 'to the owner'

17. comedendum − gerundive (see Appendix) agreeing with
    canem, 'the dog to-be-eaten'

18. capitis ossibus appensis − ablative absolute (see Appendix)
    ossibus appensis (from *appendo*) + genitive of *caput*, 'head' − they
    discarded the hide with the skull still attached

19. pedes quidam − 'a certain foot-soldier'

20. incidit − 'happens upon, stumbles upon', the preposition *in*
    reinforces the meaning; *abiectam* and *refertam* are both perfect
    participles agreeing with *pellem*: from *abicio*, 'throw away' and
    refercio, 'fill with'

21. semifetente – adverb formed from adding *semi-*, 'half', to present participle of *feteo*, 'stink' (English 'fetid'): 'half-putrid'

22. domum asportavit – *domum* is locative, 'carried it back home'

23. excussis vermibus – another ablative absolute; *excutio*, 'shake off'

24. coquendam – gerundive, 'to be cooked', from verb *coquo*; *coctam* is the perfect participle of the same verb. This sentence *excussis … edit* has a comic-poetical ring to it

25. adcoctae pellis ius – *ad + coquo* intensifies the verb, 'the juice (or broth) of the cooked hide'; *ius* is neuter accusative

26. multi … accurrebant – *multi* is the subject, they come running with their *paropsides* ('dishes') for the broth

27. singulos … pro singulis … offerentes – *singuli*, 'one each' is plural: 'offering each a gold castellan for each bowl'.

2. *Nicolaus Copernicus (1473–1543)*

Copernicus' *De revolutionibus orbium coelestium* (1543) expounds a heliocentric theory of planetary revolution, as opposed to the ancient earth-centred Ptolemaic system. Although Copernicus was wrong – planets do not revolve around the sun in perfectly spherical orbits – his revolutionary book brought about a major advancement in science. Initially the Catholic Church took no notice, but when Copernican scholars like Galileo (see below) began to support the heliocentric theory with telescopic observations, the Church reacted: in 1616 the book was 'suspended' until it could be 'corrected' – the unexpurgated first edition remained prohibited until 1835.

THE SPHERICAL UNIVERSE

At the beginning of the first book, Copernicus expatiates on why he thinks the universe is spherical in nature:

Quod mundus sit sphaericus.
Principio advertendum nobis est, globulum esse mundum, sive quod ipsa forma perfectissima sit omnium, nulla indigens compagine, tota integra; sive quod ipsa capacissima sit figurarum, quae compraehensurum omnia, et conservaturum

*maxime decet; sive etiam quod absolutissimae quaeque mundi partes, Solem
dico, Lunam et stellas, tali forma conspiciantur; sive quod hac universa appetat
terminari, quod in aquae guttis caeterisque liquidis corporibus apparet, dum
per se terminari cupiunt. Quo minus talem formam coelestibus corporibus
attributam quisquam dubitaverit.*

Notes:

1. quod ... sit – subjunctive *sit* because *quod* is introducing a
   theoretical proposition (i.e. not a factual statement), though
   Copernicus intends to demonstrate its truth subsequently.
   'That the universe is spherical'
2. principio – adverb, 'in the first place'
3. advertendum est nobis – gerundive of obligation (see
   Appendix), 'we must observe/point out'
4. globulum esse mundum – accusative + infinitive (see
   Appendix)
5. sive quod ... sive quod ... sive etiam quod – 'whether because
   ... or because ... or even because'
6. nulla ... compagine – *indigens*, 'needing, requiring' (present
   participle of *indigeo*) is followed by the ablative of *compages*,
   'structure, framework'
7. compraehensurum ... conservaturum – in the original text
   these are written as *compraehensurū ... conservaturū*, future
   participles to express purpose (see Appendix), sc. *esse* after
   impersonal verb *decet*, literally: 'that which (*quae*, i.e. the *figura*)
   best (*maxime*) suits everything (*omnia*) to be enclosed and
   maintained', i.e. 'the shape which is best suited to enclosing
   and maintaining everything'; *absolutissimae ... partes* – 'the
   most self-contained parts'
8. tali forma – ablative; *conspiciantur* – passive subjunctive from
   conspicio, 'are observed'
9. terminari – passive infinitive, 'to be bounded'
10. quod ... apparet – 'which is apparent'; *in aquae guttis* – 'in
    drops of water'
11. per se – 'through their own agency, effort', i.e. they naturally
    form themselves into a spherical shape
12. quo minus – or *quominus*, 'that ... not'; *quisquam* after *quominus*
    = 'not anyone', i.e. no one; *dubitaverit* – perfect subjunctive in
    quominus clause

13. coelestibus corporibus – dative; *attributam* (from *attribuo*),
'assigned, alloted (to)'.

3. *Thomas More (1478–1535)*

As Henry VIII's Lord Chancellor, Thomas More was given the task
of assisting the King to break away from the Church of Rome to
facilitate his divorce from Catherine of Aragon. But More's religious
principles proved stronger than his allegiance to the throne, and he was
executed for treason in 1535. Exactly four hundred years later he was
canonised by the Roman Catholic
Church. More is the subject of
Robert Bolt's play (and later film)
A Man for All Seasons.

More was a man of literature as
well as politics; he was a great friend
of Erasmus (Chapter 5), who often
stayed with More during his visits
to England. More's most famous
work is *Utopia*, written in 1516,
which – inspired by Plato's *Republic*
– is cast in the form of a dialogue
between More, another friend, and a
traveller called Raphael Hythloday.
Hythloday claims to have travelled
to the New World with Amerigo
Vespucci and discovered an island
called Utopia (from the Greek
ou, 'not' and *topos*, 'place', i.e. 'no-
place'), in which the inhabitants
have developed an ideal political
constitution. The book's full title
is *De Optimo Republicae Statu deque
Nova Insula Utopia*, 'on the best state
of a republic and the new island
utopia'.

Humanism

The term 'humanism' derives
from the *studia humanitas*, the
liberal arts or 'humanities' of
the educational curriculum.
In the revival of Classical
learning during the
fourteenth century a new
emphasis was placed on
studying the original texts
of Greek and Latin authors.
In these texts, it was argued,
could be found principles
of logic, ethics and natural
philosophy superior to
anything medieval Europe
had produced. One of the
leading lights of humanism
was Petrarch, who helped
reintroduce Ciceronian
Classical Latin (Chapter 5).
Although humanist thinking
encouraged a belief in free
will and individualism, it was
not necessarily incompatible
with Church doctrine: both
Erasmus and Thomas More
were humanists as well as
being men of the Church.

A DESCRIPTION OF UTOPIA

Insula civitates habet quattuor et quinquaginta spatiosas omnes ac magnificas,
lingua, moribus, institutis, legibus, prorsus iisdem, idem situs omnium, eadem
ubique quatenus per locum licet, rerum facies. Harum quae proximae inter se
sunt milia quattuor ac viginti separant. Nulla rursus est tam deserta, e qua non
ad aliam urbem pedibus queat unius itinere diei perveniri. Cives quaque ex urbe
terni senes ac rerum periti tractatum de rebus insulae communibus, quotannis
conveniunt nam Amaurotum – ea urbs quod tamquam in umbilico terrae
sita maxime iacet omnium partium legatis opportuna – prima, princepsque
habetur. Agri ita commode civitatibus assignati sunt, ut ab nulla parte minus
soli quam duodecim passuum milia una quaevis habeat. Ab aliqua multo
etiam amplius, videlicet qua parte longius urbes inter se disiunguntur. Nulli
urbi cupido promovendorum finium. Quippe quos habent agricolas magis
eorum se, quam dominos putant.

Notes:

1. lingua, moribus, institutis, legibus – ablatives; *prorsus iisdem,*
   'entirely the same (in respect of) language …'
2. quatenus per locum licet – 'as far as the location permits'
3. rerum facies – 'the appearance of things'
4. harum quae proximae inter se sunt – 'of those which are
   nearest to each other'
5. pedibus – 'on foot'
6. queat … perveniri – 'it may not be reached by the journey
   of one day (*unius itinere diei*)'; *perveniri* is the passive infinitive
   of pervenio, typically followed by *ad* + accusative (*ad alia*
   urbem)
7. cives … terni senes ac rerum periti – 'three senior citizens
   skilled in business'; adjective *periti* takes the genitive, *rerum*
8. tractatum … conveniunt – the supine can be used to express
   purpose after verbs of motion, here 'to deliberate, consult'
   (from *tracto*)
9. quotannis – adverb, 'annually'
10. Amaurotum – subject of *prima, princepsque habetur,* 'is regarded
    as the first and principal (city)'
11. tamquam in umbilico terra sita – *tamquam* 'as if' or 'as it were';
    in umbilico, 'in the navel', i.e. the centre
12. iacet … opportuna – 'lies in an opportune position'

13. agri ... assignati sunt – perfect passive, 'have been allotted'; *commode* – adverb, 'appropriately'

14. ut ... habeat – *ut* + subjunctive (see Appendix), 'so that from no part does any possess ...'; *minus soli quam* – literally 'less of cultivated land than'; *duodecim passuum milia* – 'twelve miles'

15. una quaevis – 'any (whichever you please)', referring to each city

16. multo etiam amplius – literally, 'greater by much'

17. longius urbes inter se disiunguntur – 'cities separated further from each other'

18. nulli urbi cupido promovendorum finium – dative of possession *cupido* sc. *est*, 'no city is desirous (of); *promovendorum* – gerund from *promoveo*, 'extend'

19. quippe – introducing an accusative + infinitive: 'indeed they consider that they are (*se putant*) more tenants (*magis agricolas*) than owners (*quam dominos*) of those territories which they possess (*quos habent eorum*)'.

4. William Camden (1551–1623)

William Camden was a remarkable scholar by the standards of any age. His *Britannia* (1586) is a monumental study of the British Isles, part-geographical, part-historical, part-antiquarian, in which England, Wales, Scotland and Ireland are described in minute detail (each county of England and Wales has its own chapter). Whenever he could, Camden travelled to the places he wrote about to see them first hand, and though his book is replete with learned quotations from authors both ancient and modern, he did not accept their testimony without corroborative evidence. *Britannia* was the first work to provide a comprehensive topographical as well as historical survey of Britain: it is still an important reference work for scholars today. It had already run to seven editions in its original Latin before an English version appeared in 1610.

A DESCRIPTION OF OXFORD

Ubi vero [Cherewellum] cum Iside confluit et amoenissimae insulae aquarum divortiis sparguntur, in campestri planitie eminet celeberrima academia Oxonia, Saxonice Oxenford, vulgo Oxford, Athenae nostrae nobilissimae,

Angliae μυσειον *et* ἐρεισμα, *imo sol, oculus, et anima, literarum et sapientiae clarissima scaturigo, unde religio, humanitas, et doctrina in omnes regni partes uberrime diffunduntur. Urbs egregia et nitida sive privatorum aedificiorum elegantiam, sive publicorum dignitatem, sive situs salubritatem et amoenitatem spectes. Planitiem enim ita obvallant nemorosi colles ut hinc pestilenti Austro, illinc tempestuoso Zephiro excluso, tantum serenantem Eurum et Aquilonem corruptionis vindicem admittant, unde ob hoc situ* Bellositum *quondam dictum fuisse produnt scriptores. Nonnulli hanc* Caer Vortigern *et* Caer Vember *Britannice appellant, et nescio quos Vortigernos et Mempricios extruxisse opinantur. Quodcunque vero Britannicis temporibus fuerit,* Saxones Oxenford *dixerunt, et ea plane significatione quae Graeci suos* Bosphoros *et Germani suam* Ochenfurt ad Oderam *habent, a boum scilicet vado, quo etiam sensu Britannis nostris hodie* Rhid-ychen *nominatur. Lelandus tamen probabili coniectura ab* Ouse *fluvio, qui Latine Isis, nomen deducit, et* Ousford *vocatum fuisse arbitratur, cum insulae amnicae quas Isis hic dispergit* Ousney *dicantur.*

Notes:

1. Cherewellum – understood from the previous paragraph, the river that runs from the direction of Banbury in the north into Oxford

2. cum Iside – ablative of *Isis*, the Latin name given to the River Thames as it flows through Oxford (*Isis* perhaps being a contraction of the Latin *Tamesis*)

3. amoenissimae insulae – the adjective *amoenus,* 'pleasant' (here in the superlative) is used when referring to nature

4. sparguntur – passive of *spargo, spargere,* 'scatter', referring to the islands which are spread about by the parting (ablative *divortiis,* from *divortium*) of the waters (*aquarum,* genitive plural)

5. academia Oxonia – literally, 'Oxonian academy', i.e. the University of Oxford

6. Saxonice ... vulgo – adverbs, 'in the Saxon tongue ... in the common tongue (i.e. in the vernacular)'

7. Athenae – in Latin Athens is a plural noun, hence adjectives *nostrae nobilissimae*

8. Angliae – not nominative plural like *Athenae* but genitive singular of *Anglia*

9. μυσεῖον *et* ἐρεισμα – Greek, take with *Angliae: mouseion,* 'the

temple of the Muses' (whence English 'museum') and *ereisma*, 'a pillar, prop'

10. imo – more regularly *immo*, 'rather'

11. scaturigo – more regularly *scaturrigo*, 'a bubbling spring' (feminine, hence adjective *clarissima*)

12. diffunduntur – passive of *diffundo*, 'spread' (English, 'diffused')

13. sive ... spectes – 'whether you look upon/admire ...'; *spectes* is subjunctive (of *specto, spectare*) because the clause is hypothetical

14. obvallant – subject is the *nemorosi colles*, 'wooded hills'; translate as 'the wooded hills protect like a wall'

15. hinc ... illinc – 'on one side ... on the other'

16. Austro ... Zephiro ... Eurum ... Aquilonem – South, West, East and North winds; the construction *Austro ... Zephiro excluso* is ablative absolute (see Appendix)

17. tantum – adverb, 'only'

18. admittant – the subjunctive verb following *obvallant nemorosi colles ut* ... (see Appendix for *ut* + subjunctive)

19. vindicem corruptionis – 'protector from disease', *vindex* + genitive of the thing from which protection is given

20. ob hoc situ – *ob*, 'because of' + ablative

21. Bellositum – 'Lovely place'; English word-order here is: *scriptores produnt fuisse quondam dictum Bellositum* – the construction after *produnt* (from *prodo*, 'publish, record') is accusative + infinitive (see Appendix): *fuisse dictum*, 'had been called'

22. nonnulli hanc ... appellant ... opinantur – 'some (writers) call this ... are of the opinion/suppose ...'; *opinor* is deponent not passive

23. *Britannice* – adverb, 'in the British (i.e. Welsh) language'

24. nescio quos – 'some (unknown) ones', literally the phrase means 'I don't know what'; translate here as 'who knows what'

25. Vortigernos et Mempricios – accusative plurals following accusative + infinitive construction *extruxisse opinantur* (see Appendix). Vortigern is attested by Gildas in his *De Excidio et Conquestu Britanniae* ('On the Ruin and Conquest of Britain') in the sixth century; Mempricus is a more shadowy figure,

reputed to be the father of Ebraucus the founder of York (Latin *Eboracum*)

26. quodcunque – more regularly *quodcumque*, 'whatever'; *Britannicis temporibus* – 'in British times', i.e. before the invasions of the Angles and Saxons; *fuerit* – perfect subjunctive of *sum*, 'it may have been (called)'

27. ea plane significatione … Ochenfurt ad Oderam – *plane* is the adverb; a full translation would be something like 'and evidently (they meant) by that designation what the Greeks have by their Bosphorus and the Germans their Ochenfurt-upon-Oder'

28. a boum … vado – 'a ford for oxen'; *boum* is genitive plural of *bos, bovis* (English 'bovine'); the preposition *a* goes with ablative *vado*, literally 'from the ford of oxen'

29. quo sensu – 'in which sense/meaning'; *etiam … hodie* – 'even today'; *nominatur* – passive, 'is called', hence ablative *Britannis nostris* – 'by our (native) Britons (i.e. the Welsh)'

30. Lelandus – antiquarian scholar John Leland (1506-1552) whose *Itinerary* of England and Wales was the forerunner of Camden's own book

31. probabili coniectura – ablative, 'by a reasonable inference'

32. Latine – adverb, 'in Latin'

33. Ousford vocatum fuisse arbitratur – accusative + infinitive following *arbitratur*

34. cum … dicantur – *cum* + passive subjunctive, here = 'since they are called …'; *insulae amnicae* - 'the river islands'

5. Galileo Galilei (1564-1642)

Italian scientist Galileo Galilei has been called, *inter alia*, the father of modern astronomy and the father of modern science. An ardent supporter of heliocentricism (see above), he used a new-fangled device called a telescope (*perspicillus*) to make empirical observations which helped to confirm Copernicus' theory. Sadly, he was later forced by the Inquisition to recant and was placed under house arrest until he died.

THE MOONS OF JUPITER

In his book *Sidereus Nuncius* ('the starry messenger') Galileo describes how, early in the year 1610, he used his telescope to observe four moons (*Erraticas Stellas*, 'wandering stars') moving in circular orbits around Jupiter:

Verum, quod omnem admirationem longe superat, quodve admonitos faciendos cunctos Astronomos atque Philosophos nos apprime impulit, illud est, quod scilicet quatuor Erraticas Stellas, nemini eorum qui ante nos cognitas aut observatas, adinvenimus, quae circa Stellam quandam insignem e numero cognitarum, instar Veneris atque Mercurii circa Solem, suas habent periodos, eamque modo praeeunt, modo subsequuntur, nunquam extra certos limites ab illa digredientes. Quae omnia ope Perspicilli a me excogitati, divina prius illuminante gratia, paucis abhinc diebus, reperta atque observata fuerunt.

Notes:

1. verum, quod – Galileo is continuing his introductory remarks about what revelations the book contains: 'But, that which ...'

2. longe superat – imperfect of *supersum* with adverb *longe*: 'was far surpassing'

3. admonitos faciendos ... impulit – the gerundive *faciendos* plus noun *admonitos* after a verb of undertaking or entrusting (here *impello*): translate as 'urged us to make aware' (see Appendix)

4. cunctos – 'all the others', i.e. excepting himself

5. nos – as is frequent in Latin the first-person plural is used by the writer in referring to himself, where in modern English we tend to prefer the singular

6. Erraticas Stellas – not a new coinage but a phrase from Classical sources

7. nemini eorum qui ante nos – literally 'by none of those who (came) before us', i.e. previous astronomers and philosophers; in English better to make it positive, 'not observed ... by any of those'

8. adinvenimus – 'discovered in addition', i.e. 'I have also discovered ...'; *quae* – relative pronoun referring to *stellas*

9. stellam quandam insignem – 'a certain visible (or bright) star' i.e. Jupiter; as Galileo's choice of words indicates, the modern

distinction between planets and stars was not yet clear

10. instar – 'after the fashion of, like' + genitive of *Venus* and *Mercurius*

11. suas ... periodos – 'their own circuits' i.e. 'orbits'

12. modo ... modo – 'at one time ... at another'

13. eamque – accusative pronoun from *ea*, referring to the *stellam* (Jupiter)

14. *praeeunt* – from *praeeo* (*prae* + *eo*), 'go before, precede'; *subsequuntur* – deponent, 'follow after'; as Jupiter moves across the night sky, the satellites seem at one time to be moving in front of it, at another following it

15. digredientes – present participle from *digredior*, 'deviating'

16. ope – ablative of *ops* + genitive, 'by means of/by the help of'

17. Perspicilli – genitive of *Perspicillus*, 'telescope', a new coinage for a new device, derived from the verb *perspicere*, 'to see through'

18. *excogitati* – genitive in agreement with *perspicilli*, 'invented'

19. divina ... gratia – ablative, 'by divine grace'

20. paucis abhinc diebus – ablative of time when the event occurred, 'a few days ago'

21. reperta ... observata – perfect passive participles (from *reperio* and *observo*) agreeing with *omnia*.

6. René Descartes (1596–1650)

Often referred to as the father of Western Philosophy, René Descartes is best known for a bold thought-experiment in which he set out to discover what knowledge, if any, rested on firm foundations by trying to doubt the existence of everything. This was revolutionary because Descartes was refusing to accept any previous authorities (specifically Aristotle, whose syllogistic logic was the *sine qua non* of scholastic reasoning), deciding instead to go right back to first principles. He expounded the concept in French in *Discours de la Méthode,* published in 1637, but it was not until four years later with the publication in Latin of his *Meditationes* (1641) that his methods caught the attention of scholars across Europe.

(i) The Method of Doubt

In the First Meditation, Descartes carries out his Method of Doubt: can he find anything at all of which he is absolutely certain? On reflection he realises that the existence of all external things – of objects, other people, even his own body – cannot be ascertained with complete confidence, since although he believes he is now sitting at his desk, he could in fact be asleep and dreaming. Worse, he could be being deceived by some malicious demon:

The title page of the 1641 edition reads: *Meditationes De Prima Philosophia, in Qua Dei Existentia et Animae Immortalitas Demonstratur*, 'Meditations on the First Philosophy, in which the existence of God and of a soul distinct from the body is demonstrated'.

Later editions have the slightly different: *Meditationes De Prima Philosophia, In quibus Dei Existentia, & Animae humanae a corpore Distinctio, demonstrantur*, 'Meditations on the First Philosophy, in which the existence of God and of a human spirit distinct from the body are demonstrated'.

Supponam igitur non optimum Deum, fontem veritatis, sed genium aliquem malignum, eundemque summe potentem et callidum, omnem suam industriam in eo posuisse, ut me falleret: putabo coelum, aërem, terram, colores, figuras, sonos, cunctaque externa nihil aliud esse quam ludificationes somniorum, quibus insidias credulitati meae tetendit: considerabo meipsum tanquam manus non habentem, non oculos, non carnem, non sanguinem, non aliquem sensum, sed haec omnia me habere falsò opinantem: manebo obstinate in hac meditatione defixus, atque ita, siquidem non in potestate mea sit aliquid veri cognoscere, at certe hoc quod in me est, ne falsis assentiar, nec mihi quidquam iste deceptor, quantumvis potens, quantumvis callidus, possit imponere, obfirmata mente cavebo.

Notes:

1. supponam – subjunctive of *suppono*, 'let me suppose (that) …'
2. optimum Deum … posuisse – accusative + infinitive (see Appendix)
3. genium – the *genius* was, for the Romans, a protecting deity (Christianised as a guardian angel), but here it is a malignant force

4. summe – adverb, 'in the highest degree'

5. in eo – 'in the circumstance/matter'

6. posuisse – perfect infinitive, 'had applied, brought to bear'

7. ut me falleret – *ut* + subjunctive (see Appendix), 'in order to deceive me'

8. putabo coelum … esse – accusative + infinitive after *putabo*, 'I will consider that the sky … is nothing other than', though English could equally well translate from the Latin as, 'I will regard the sky … to be nothing other than'

9. ludificationes – 'triflings', i.e. delusions

10. quibus – relative pronoun referring to the *ludificationes*

11. insidias … tetendit – 'laid snares'; *credulitati meae* is dative of disadvantage

12. tanquam – or *tamquam*, 'in the same way'

13. haec omnia … opinantem – *opinantem* is, like *habentem* before, governed by *considerabo*: 'I will consider myself as not having … as falsely imagining', followed by an accusative + infinitive *haec omnia me habere*, 'that I have all these things'

14. obstinante – adverb

15. defixus – perfect participle passive (see Appendix) from *defigo*, 'fix'

16. siquidem – 'if at any rate', subjunctive *sit* because a hypothetical clause

17. aliquid veri cognoscere – genitive of *verum* after *aliquid*, literally 'something of truth' = 'anything true'

18. hoc quod in me est – literally 'this thing (*hoc*), which (*quod*) is in me (i.e. in my power)'

19. ne falsis assentiar – negative *ne* + subjunctive (see Appendix: *ut* + subjunctive)

20. nec … imponere – take *possit imponere* after subject *iste deceptor* (*iste* has a pejorative connotation): 'nor may that deceiver impose anything on me' – *imponere mihi*, 'to trick, deceive, impose upon me'

21. obfirmata mente – ablative absolute (see Appendix); *cavebo* – future tense.

(ii) *Cogito ergo sum*

After thus wrecking the foundations of knowledge, in the Second Meditation, Descartes begins to rebuild them on a surer footing – the certainty of his own existence:

Sed mihi persuasi nihil plane esse in mundo, nullum coelum, nullam terram, nullas mentes, nulla corpora; nonne igitur etiam me non esse? Imo certe ego eram, si quid mihi persuasi. Sed est deceptor nescio quis, summe potens, summe callidus, qui de industria me semper fallit. Haud dubie igitur ego etiam sum, si me fallit; & fallat quantum potest, nunquam tamen efficiet, ut nihil sim quamdiu me aliquid esse cogitabo. Adeo ut, omnibus satis superque pensitatis, denique statuendum sit hoc pronuntiatum, Ego sum, ego existo, quoties a me profertur, vel mente concipitur, necessario esse verum.

Notes:
1. Cogito ergo sum – the famous tag actually occurs in the *Discourse on Method* of 1637, not in the Latin version
2. mihi persuasi – 'I persuaded myself', (*persuadeo* takes the dative, hence *mihi*); *nihil esse* is accusative + infinitive (see Appendix), though *nihil* is indeclinable; *esse* – 'to be' but also 'exist'
3. nonne – introduces a question that expects the answer 'yes'
4. ego eram – 'I existed'
5. deceptor nescio quis – 'some (unknown) deceiver'; *summe* – adverb, 'in the highest degree'
6. de industria – 'diligently'
7. haud dubie – 'indisputably'
8. fallat – 'jussive' subjunctive: 'let him deceive me'
9. efficiet – future; *ut ... sim* – *ut* + subjunctive (see Appendix)
10. quamdiu – 'so long as'; *me aliquid esse* – accusative + infinitive after *cogitabo*, future
11. adeo ut ... statuendum sit – *ut* + subjunctive; *statuendum* is gerundive (see Appendix): 'so that it must be established ...'; *omnibus pensitatis*, 'with all things considered,' *satis superque*, 'more than sufficiently'
12. hoc pronuntiatum ... necessario esse verum – accusative + infinitive after *statuendum sit*: 'that this proposition is necessarily true'
13. profertur – passive of *profero*, 'make known, utter'.

Recommended Reading:

William Camden   *Britannia*
                                      George Olms

A facsimile reprint of the 1607 Latin edition of Camden's *magnum opus*.

Peter Martyr (ed. Eatough)   *Selections from Peter Martyr*
                                  (De Orbe Novo, **Book I)**
                                  Brepols

Despite the prosaic title this is the complete text of the first *Decade* of Martyr's *De Orbe Novo*, with an English translation and comprehensive textual and historical commentary by Geoffrey Eatough.

Martyr (ed. Iacona & George) *Columbus' First Voyage*
                                 Bolchazy-Carducci

For those who first want to dip their toes into Martyr, so to speak: a slim paperback with five short passages from Martyr's first *Decade* intended specifically as translation exercises for students.

Thomas More (ed. Lupton) *Utopia*
                              Kessinger Publishing

The Latin text of 1518, together with the 1551 English translation by Ralph Robynson.

English translations:

Copernicus (trans. Wallis)   Prometheus Books

Descartes (trans. Sutcliffe)   Penguin Classics

Galileo (trans. van Helden)   University of Chicago Press

More (trans. Turner)   Penguin Classics

CHAPTER 7

NEO-LATIN POETRY

> Poets that lasting Marble seek
> Must carve in *Latine* or in *Greek,*
> We write in Sand, our language grows,
> And like the Tide our work o'erflows.
>
> (Edmund Waller, *Of English Verse*)

In these lines Edmund Waller makes the point that if a writer wishes his work to be permanent he should not write in the vernacular but choose Latin or Greek instead, since the ancient languages are permanent while our native tongues change from generation to generation. 'Chaucer his Sense can only boast / The glory of his numbers lost', Waller continues. We might add the same is true even for Shakespeare, whose English is so different from our current idiom that it must be laboriously explained to each new generation of schoolchildren almost as if it were a foreign language.

Waller's lesson has been forgotten in modern times, but it was not lost on his contemporaries. D.K. Money in his book *The English Horace* estimates the number of Neo-Latin poets in Britain alone between 1550 and 1750 at 10,000. It is only comparatively recently that the ability to compose both prose and poetry in Latin has been entirely neglected: the argument presumably being that there's no benefit in attempting to express your thoughts in a 'dead' language – though given that, as we have discovered, Latin was the dominant language of discourse across Europe for almost 2000 years, such an attitude seems a little short-sighted.

> 'It may be that few modern authors are quite as good as Virgil or Horace; few ancient authors were, either. Good modern authors are better than mediocre ancient ones.'
> (D.K. Money, *The English Horace*)

A MISCELLANY OF NEO-LATIN POETS

1. *Desiderius Erasmus (c.1466/9-1536)*

This youthful 'querulous elegy' dates from around the time when the teenage Erasmus entered the monastery at Steyn in *c.*1487. It is the complaint of a young man who thinks he is burdened with the disabilities of old age. Erasmus also features in Chapter 5.

Elegia Erasmi: Querula Doloris

> *Cum nondum albenti surgant mihi vertice cani,*
>   *Candeat aut pilis frons viduata suis,*
> *Luminibusve hebet aciem numerosior aetas,*
>   *Aut dens squalenti decidat ore niger,*
> *Atque acuant rigidae nondum mihi bracchia setae, aut*
>   *Pendeat arenti corpore laxa cutis,*
> *Denique nulla meae videam argumenta senectae,*
>   *Nescio quid misero sorsque deusque parent.*
> *Me mala ferre senum teneris voluere sub annis,*
>   *Iamque senem esse volunt, nec senuisse sinunt.*
> *Iam quae canitie spergant mea tempora tristi,*
>   *Praevenere diem cura dolorque suum.*

Notes:

1. Metre: elegiac couplets (see Chapter 3). The text can be found in the Supplement to the *Opera Omnia Desiderii Erasmi* published by George Olms

2. *querula* agrees with *elegia* – 'An elegy … full of complaints'; *Erasmi* and *doloris* are both genitive, take the former after *elegia*, the latter after *querula*

3. cum … surgant – *cum* followed by the present subjunctive can mean 'since' or 'although' – we want the latter here, as the completion of the sentence in line 8 reveals the sense is: 'Although I show no visible signs of growing old, some unknown fortune and god subject me to their will'

4. cani – nominative plural, 'grey hairs', the subject of *surgant* (here = 'grow'); *canus* can mean 'white' but also 'white or grey-haired'

5. albenti … vertice – ablative, literally, 'on the whitening crown': *vertex* = 'top of the head'; *albens* = 'becoming white (with age)' – the present participle ablative singular ends in −*e* except when used as an adjective

6. candeat – 'glisten', present subjunctive, subject is *frons*, 'forehead'

7. viduata – perfect participle passive, feminine agreeing with *frons*, of *viduo* + ablative (here *pilis suis*, 'its own hairs') = '(having been) deprived of …'

8. luminibusve – *lumen*, 'light', is often used poetically instead of *oculus*, 'eye'; *luminibus* is ablative of respect after *aciem*, literally: 'the keenness (in respect of) my eyes'; the enclitic −*ve* = 'or'

9. numerosior aetas – comparative of *numerosus*: 'a more abundant (i.e. older) age'

10. hebet – all the other verbs in lines 1-7 are subjunctive (after *cum* in line 1: 'Although neither this nor that nor the other is the case') but *hebet*, 'blunts' or 'dulls', is indicative: possibly a mistake?

11. dens … niger – 'black teeth', the inevitable result of growing old in an age without high standards of dental hygiene; *decidat* – present subjunctive, 'fall'

12. squalenti … ore – *squalere* can be 'dirty, unkempt' (English 'squalid') or figuratively 'barren' – either use would fit here; *squalenti* is another ablative present participle ending in −*i* as it qualifies *ore*, 'mouth'

13. rigidae … setae – nominative plural, 'stiff bristles'; *seta* is more normally spelt *saeta*, 'rough hair'; subject of subjunctive verb *acuant*, 'make sharp': an old man's hairs make his arms feel bristly

14. bracchia – accusative plural, 'arms', translate *mihi* as *mea*

15. pendeat – subjunctive again, 'hang down' (English 'pendant'); subject is *laxa cutis*, 'loose skin'

16. arenti corpore – the same construction of present participle ablative qualifying a noun: *arens* = 'dry', 'withered'

17. denique … senectae – 'in short I can see no proof (*nulla argumenta*) of my growing old (*meae senectae*)'

18. nescio quid … parent – the climax of this long first sentence, some unknown (*nescio quid*) fortune (*sors*) and god (*deus*) are attending (*parent*) to the unfortunate Erasmus (*misero*)

19. me ... ferre ... voluere – accusative + infinitive (see Appendix) after *voluere*, a contraction for *voluerunt* (perfect tense): 'they desired that I bear the evils of old men (*mala senum*) in the time of my tender (i.e. youthful) years (*teneris ... sub annis*)'

20. senem esse volunt – another accusative + infinitive after *volunt* (present tense); also for *senuisse sinunt* – understand *me* as the accusative subject of *senuisse*: 'nor do they allow that I had grown old'

21. iam ... dolorque suum – the final couplet reveals the source of Erasmus' complaint: the subjects *cura dolorque* ('worry and pain') are delayed right until the end; *quae* in the penultimate line refers to them: 'which shower my life (*mea tempora*) with sad old age (*canitie tristi*)'; *canities* (like *cani* in line 1) can mean 'grey or white hair' as well as 'old age'

22. praevenere – a contraction for *praevenerunt*, 'they have arrived ahead of... '; *diem ... suum* – 'their (appointed) day'.

2. *John Milton (1608–1674)*

Much of Milton's early poetry is in Latin: from academic exercises to epistolary elegies addressed to his friend Charles Diodati. One substantial student piece is *In Quintum Novembris* ('on the fifth of November'), a popular subject of the time – a few years earlier Thomas Campion (1567-1620) had written a lengthy poem called *De Pulverea Coniuratione* ('On the Gunpowder Plot'), and as late as 1735 Thomas Gray was still writing about Guy Fawkes (see below). In Milton's collected poems of 1645, there are a group of short epigrams on the same theme, beginning with this one:

(i) *In proditionem Bombardicam*

> *Cum simul in regem nuper satrapasque Britannos*
>   *Ausus es infandum perfide Fauxe nefas,*
> *Fallor? an et mitis voluisti ex parte videri,*
>   *Et pensare mala cum pietate scelus;*
> *Scilicet hos alti missurus ad atria cæli,*
>   *Sulphureo curru flammivolisque rotis.*
> *Qualiter ille feris caput inviolabile Parcis*
>   *Liquit Jordanios turbine raptus agros.*

Notes:

1. Metre: elegiac couplets (see Chapter 3)

2. Bombardicam – *pulvis bombardica* is a neo-Latin coinage for something unknown to the ancients: 'gunpowder'

3. cum simul – 'when at the same time'

4. in regem – *in* + accusative meaning 'against'

5. satrapasque Britannos – a satrap was a provincial governor in the Persian empire (*satrapes, satrapae*, masculine); Milton means Parliament

6. ausus es – perfect of deponent *audeo*, 'dare', 'attempt', 'venture upon'

7. perfide Fauxe – vocative

8. fallor – passive of *fallo*: 'am I deceived/mistaken?'

9. an – introduces the second part of the question. The punctuation is a bit misleading here: translate, 'am I mistaken or did you wish to seem …?'

10. mitis – 'soft' or 'merciful'

11. ex parte – 'partly' or 'to some extent'

12. pensare – 'to compensate for', followed by *cum* + ablative

13. mala – the scansion reveals that the final 'a' falls on the 2½ foot of the pentameter, making it long: *malā* thus ablative in agreement with *pietate*, 'wicked piety'

14. scilicet – introduces a clause specifying Fawkes' criminal intention; *hos* refers to the king and Parliament

15. missurus – future participle of *mitto*, expressing purpose (see Appendix): he intends to send them from the Palace of Westminster to the palace (*ad atria*) of high heaven (*alti caeli*)

16. sulphureo curru – sulphur is an ingredient of gunpowder; *flammivolis* – an adjective from *flamma* + *volo*, 'flying with flames'; the metaphor is biblical, alluded to in the final couplet

17. qualiter ille – the comparison is between Fawkes and the prophet Elijah, who was taken up (*raptus*) to heaven by a whirlwind (*turbine*) after a chariot of fire drawn by fiery horses had appeared to him beside the River Jordan (*Jordanios agros*) – see 2 *Kings* 2:11; Milton suggests this was the biblical precedent Fawkes had in mind

18. caput inviolabile – his 'untouchable head', i.e. he being favoured by God was not subject to the decrees of the fierce Fates (*feris Parcis*).

A more attractive subject is Milton's admiration of the Neapolitan singer
Leonora Baroni, whom the poet heard at the Roman palace of Cardinal
Barberini in 1638. Below is the first of three short poems about her.

(ii) *Ad Leonoram Romæ canentem*

> *Angelus unicuique suus (sic credite gentes)*
> *Obtigit æthereis ales ab ordinibus.*
> *Quid mirum? Leonora tibi si gloria maior,*
> *Nam tua præsentem vox sonat ipsa Deum.*
> *Aut Deus, aut vacui certe mens tertia cœli*
> *Per tua secreto guttura serpit agens;*
> *Serpit agens, facilisque docet mortalia corda*
> *Sensim immortali assuescere posse sono.*
> *Quod si cuncta quidem Deus est, per cunctaque fusus,*
> *In te una loquitur, cætera mutus habet.*

Notes:

1. Metre: elegiac couplets (see Chapter 3)
2. angelus suus ales – everyone has been assigned a guardian
    angel; *obtigit* – perfect of *obtingo*, 'falls to one's lot'; *unicuique*
    – dative of *unusquisque*, 'to everyone'
3. sic credite gentes – *credite* is imperative, which makes *gentes*
    vocative: 'believe it is so, ye nations'
4. quid mirum – 'what a marvel', but the question being directed
    at Leonora invites us to translate: 'why wonder, Leonora, if
    you have …?'
5. praesentem Deum – 'your voice declares (*sonat*) the presence
    of God'
6. aut … aut – 'either … or'
7. mens tertia – 'the third mind', Milton is perhaps thinking of
    the Holy Spirit here
8. vacui coeli – heaven is empty because God/the Holy Spirit
    has come down to inhabit Leonora's throat!
9. serpit agens – *ago* is a handily vague verb, here probably
    meaning 'moving, directing' or 'giving utterance' via Leonora;
    serpo means 'creep, crawl' (English 'serpent'), hence 'insinuate';
    repetition of the phrase is an example of a rhetorical technique
    called anaphora

10. facilisque – a Latin adjective can sometimes be better translated by an English adverb, so here 'easily'

11. docet ... assuescere posse – accusative + infinitive after *docet* (see Appendix); the verb after *posse* is always infinitive. *immortali ... sono* – 'that mortal hearts can become accustomed to an immortal sound'

12. quod – introducing a clause of explanation, 'because ...'

13. si cuncta ... Deus est – 'if God is everywhere'

14. fusus – perfect participle from *fundo*, 'pour out', 'emit' or 'utter'; so here, 'he has been given utterance through ...'

15. caetera mutus habet – literally, 'silent he holds/keeps the rest'; the English works better if we transfer the epithet *mutus* from *Deus* to *caetera*: 'he keeps the rest silent'.

3. Joseph Addison (1672–1719)

Addison, who along with Richard Steele, was the founder of *The Spectator*, is one of English literature's greatest essayists. But as a student at Oxford he also wrote a substantial amount of Latin verse, including comical mock-epics on the Battle of the Pygmies and Cranes (*Praelium inter Pygmaeos et Grues Commissum*), a puppet show (*Machinae Gesticulantes*) and a game of bowls (*Sphaeristerium*). Such witty flights of fancy did not endear Addison's Latin poetry to Dr Johnson (see box).

> ### Johnson on Addison's Latin
>
> 'When the matter is low or scanty, a dead language, in which nothing is mean because nothing is familiar, affords great conveniences; and by the sonorous magnificence of Roman syllables, the writer conceals penury of thought, and want of novelty, often from the reader, and often from himself.' (*Lives of the Poets*)

A Game of Bowls

An excerpt from Addison's mock-epic *Sphaeristerium* in heroic hexameters:

> *Evolat orbiculus, quae cursum meta futurum*
> *Designat; iactique legens vestigia, primam,*

Qui certamen init, sphaeram demittit, at illa
Leniter effusa, exiguum quod ducit in orbem,
Radit iter, donec sensim primo impetu fesso
Subsistat; subito globus emicat alter et alter.
Mox ubi funduntur late agmina crebra minorem
Sparsa per orbiculum, stipantque frequentia metam,
Atque negant faciles aditus; iam cautius exit,
Et leviter sese insinuat revolubile lignum.
At si forte globum, qui misit, spectat inertem
Serpere, et impressum subito languescere motum,
Pone urget sphaerae vestigia, et anxius instat,
Obiurgatque moras, currentique imminet orbi.
Atque ut segnis honos dextrae servetur, iniquam
Incusat terram, ac surgentem in marmore nodum.
Nec risus tacuere, globus cum volvitur actus
Infami iactu, aut nimium vestigia plumbum
Allicit, et sphaeram a recto trahit insita virtus
Tum qui proiecit, strepitus effundit inanes,
Et, variam in speciem distorto corpore, falsos
Increpat errores, et dat convitia ligno.
Sphaera sed, irarum temnens ludibria, coeptum
Pergit iter, nullisque movetur surda querelis.

Notes:

1. orbiculus – the ending – *culus* is the Latin diminutive, here of *orbis*, 'ball': the little ball in question being the jack; *evolat* – 'flies out', a compound verb from *volo, volare*, 'fly'

2. quae … meta – *metae* were the cone-shaped turning-posts at each end of the Circus Maximus in Rome and other race tracks (remember Charlton Heston's chariot race in *Ben-Hur*), but the word can also mean as here 'a marker': 'which marker traces out (*designat*) the future course (*cursum futurum*)'

3. iactique legens vestigia – *vestigia legere* means 'to follow the track of', so we can expect a word in the genitive case, here the perfect participle of *iacio*, 'throw': translate as 'following the track of the thrown (ball)'

4. primam … sphaeram – 'the first ball', *demittit* – 'he lets drop', who? *qui certamen init* – 'he who begins the contest'

5. illa leniter effusa – 'that (the ball) feebly let loose'; *effusa* is the

perfect participle passive from *effundo*

6. radit iter – 'traces a path, which (*quod*: neuter after *iter*) leads towards the small ball (*ducit in exiguum orbem*)'

7. sensim – adverb, 'gradually'; *primo impetu fesso* – ablative, 'with its first charge (*impetus*, fourth declension) exhausted stops short (*subsistat*)'

8. subito – adverb, 'suddenly'; *alter et alter emicat* – 'one after another darts forth'

9. mox ... orbiculum – English word-order: *mox agmina crebra* ('soon a tight-packed throng') *funduntur* (passive, plural because *agmina* is neuter plural, 'spread out') *sparsa* (perfect participle passive from *spargo*, 'scatter') *late* (adverb, 'widely') *per minorem orbiculum* ('around the smaller little ball')

10. frequentia – 'a dense mass', neuter plural agreeing with *agmina*; *stipant* – 'they surround'

11. faciles aditus – 'an easy approach'

12. cautius – comparative, 'more cautiously'

13. leviter sese insinuat – 'carefully (*leviter*) makes its way through' (English, 'insinuate')

14. revolubile lignum – 'revolving' or 'backwards-rolling'; *lignum* – bowls are called 'woods'

15. at ... serpere – English word-order: *at si forte qui misit spectat* ('he who sent it sees that ...') followed by accusative + infinitive *inertem globum serpere* (*serpo*, 'creep')

16. impressum ... motum – accusative + infinitive with *languescere* 'that the applied motion (*impressum* is the perfect passive participle of *imprimo*, 'apply') grows weak'

17. pone – adverb, 'from behind'; *vestigia spherae* – 'the track of the ball'

18. anxius – 'the anxious man' but translate as adverb, 'anxiously'

19. obiurgat ... moras – 'reprimands the delay'

20. currenti ... orbi – dative after intransitive verb *imminet*, 'bends over the running ball'

21. ut ... servetur – *ut* + subjunctive clause (see Appendix) = 'in order that the honour (*honos*) of his right hand (*dextrae*) is preserved'

22. iniquam ... terram – 'uneven ground'; *incusat* – 'blames'

23. surgentem ... nodum – 'an impediment arising'; *in marmore* – i.e. on the surface of the ball

24. nec risus tacuere – 'they (other players or onlookers) do not keep their laughter quiet'; *risus* – accusative plural; *tacuere* – shortened third-person plural perfect tense of *taceo* (English: 'tacit')

25. globus ... actus – 'a driven ball'; *volvitur* – passive, 'is rolled'; *infami iactu* – ablative, 'with a disgraceful throw'

26. nimium plumbum – the bias of the bowl was originally caused by adding a lead weight to one side; *vestigia allicit* – 'draws its track'

27. insita virtus – 'its innate quality' i.e. its bias; *a recto* – 'from the right (track)'

28. strepitus – accusative plural (*strepitūs*) with *inanes*, 'vain noises'

29. variam in speciem distorto corpore – 'with his body bent into various shapes'

30. falsos ... errores – 'false wanderings'; *increpat* – 'rebukes'

31. convitia – 'insults'; *ligno* – dative after *dat*

32. sphaera ... temnens ludibria ... coeptum pergit iter – 'the ball, scorning insults, carries along the route (*iter*) it has begun (*coeptum*)'

33. movetur surda – 'deaf it is moved (*movetur*, passive) *nullis querelis*, 'by no complaints'.

4. *Thomas Gray (1716–1771)*

Thomas Gray achieved instant fame with his *Elegy Written in a Country Churchyard*, first published in 1751. But he was never prolific and only published 13 poems in his lifetime. A substantial portion of his poetry is in Latin, including a lengthy didactic poem, *De Principiis Cogitandi* ('on the elements of thinking') which was unfinished at the time of his death. Gray wrote down many of his poems in his Commonplace Book, which he began while still a student at Cambridge, and to which he continued to add until the end of his life. *Farewell to Fiesole* was written in 1741 but was not published until 1775.

(i) Farewell to Fiesole

> *Oh Faesulae, amoena*
> *Frigoribus iuga, nec nimium spirantibus auris!*
> *Alma quibus Tusci Pallas decus Apennini*
> *Esse dedit, glaucaque sua canescere sylva.*

Non ego vos posthac Arni de valle videbo
Porticibus circum, et candenti cincta corona
Villarum longe nitido consurgere dorso,
Antiquamve aedem, et veteres praeferre cupressus
Mirabor, tectisque super pendentia tecta.

Notes:

1. Metre: hexameters (see Chapter 3)

2. Faesulae amoena – by a metrical sleight of hand, the diphthong –*ae*, which would make the syllable heavy, is elided with the short *a-* of *amoena*: *Faesul(ae) amoena*, making the scansion: – ˘ ˘ | – –

3. frigoribus ... auris – ablative, 'with your cooling breezes'; *spirantibus* – also referring to *auris*, 'not too blowy!'

4. Alma ... Pallas – subject of *dedit* ('bestowed, granted') followed by dative *quibus* then accusative + infinitive *decus esse*: 'that you are the splendour of the Tuscan Apennine'

5. Apennini – the first 'a' is long, making a heavy syllable, and thus the fifth foot is a spondee instead of the customary dactyl

6. glauca ... sua ... sylva – ablative; *canescere* – infinitive, 'that you become hoary with her own grey-green (*glauca*) forests'

7. Arni – genitive of *Arnus*, the river Arno. *videbo* – 'I will not see you hereafter ...'

8. circum ... cincta – both followed by ablatives; *cincta* from verb *cingo*, 'surround, girdle'; *candenti* ('glistening') is ablative of the present participle which ends in -*i* when used as an adjective

9. nitido ... dorso – ablative, 'on your shining ridge'

10. consurgere ... praeferre – infinitives functioning as nominative gerunds (see Appendix): 'rising up ... screening'

11. mirabor – future tense, 'nor will I marvel at ...'

12. tectisque – ablative; *pendentia tecta* – accusative plural after preposition *super*: 'roofs above hanging roofs'.

Gray's *In 5tam Novembris* derives from a long tradition of student exercises on the Gunpowder Plot (see also Milton above). Many of these were, unsurprisingly, virulently anti-Catholic in tone. But Gray's depiction of suicidal religious fundamentalists planting bombs in order to destroy the institutions of the state is one that, tragically, lends such antiquated poems an unexpected contemporary relevance. This extract from Gray's version begins with a characterisation of Guy Fawkes as a fifth columnist, a 'son of Albion' who nevertheless 'despises his ancestors'. The poem was written around 1735 but not published until 1884.

> ## Johnson on Gray's Latin
>
> 'His first ambition was to have excelled in Latin poetry: perhaps it were reasonable to wish that he had prosecuted his design; for though there is at present some embarrassment in his phrase, and some harshness in his Lyrick numbers, his copiousness of language is such as very few possess, and his lines, even when imperfect, discover a writer whom practice would quickly have made skilful.' (*Lives of the Poets*)

(ii) *In 5tam Novembris*

> *Ex natis surgit mens aspernata priores,*
>   *et tentare novas ingeniosa vias,*
> *Quae caecis novit Martem sepelire latebris,*
>   *tectosque a visu Solis habere dolos;*
> *Scilicet, ut fallat, non ire in viscera terrae,*
>   *non dubitat simili clade vel ipse mori.*
> *Iamque incepit opus: careat successibus, opto;*
>   *et vetet inceptum Fors, precor, istud opus:*
> *Nec frustra; effulget subito lux aurea caeli,*
>   *(aspice) rimanti dum domus atra patet;*
> *Reclusamque vides fraudem, letique labores,*
>   *antraque miraris sulphure foeta suo:*
> *Quod si venturi haec armamentaria fati*
>   *panderat haud sacri gratia dia poli;*
> *Iure scelus se iactaret, procerumque ruina*
>   *tantum una gentem perdomuisse manu.*

Notes:

1. Metre: elegiac couplets (see Chapter 3)
2. *ex natis* – 'from among the sons (of Albion)' – the achievements of Albion were the subject of the previous lines
3. *aspernata* – perfect participle active from deponent *aspernor*, 'scorn, despise', take with *mens*

4. priores – 'those who came before'

5. ingeniosa – 'naturally suited', also with *mens*

6. quae – i.e. the *mens*, 'which knows how (*novit*) to conceal (*sepelire*) Mars (metonymy for 'war') in blind hiding-places (*caecis … latebris*)'

7. habere – 'to keep plots (*dolos*) hidden (*tectos*) from the sight (*a visu*) of the Sun (*Solis*)'

8. ut fallat – *ut* + subjunctive (see Appendix), 'in order to deceive'; *non ire … dubitat*, 'he does not hesitate to go'; *in viscera terrae* – 'into the bowels of the earth'

9. ipse mori – 'to die himself in the same destruction (*simili clade*)': Guy Fawkes was a 'suicide bomber'

10. careat – present subjunctive, 'let the work (*opus*) lack a successful outcome (dative *successibus*, after intransitive verb *careo*)

11. vetet – another subjunctive expressing the hope that Chance (*Fors*) may prevent the work that has been undertaken (*inceptum opus*)

12. nec frustra – his prayers are not in vain: the dark house (*domus atra*) is revealed to an investigator (dative *rimanti* from verb *rimor*, 'examine') carrying a golden light of heaven (*lux aurea caeli*)

13. reclusam … fraudem – 'the fraud exposed (*recludo*, 'open, reveal') and the labours of death (*leti*)'

14. miraris – 'you marvel at the caves (*antra*) stinking (*foeta*) with sulphur (*sulphure*)'

15. quod … poli – subject of the verb *panderat* (pluperfect, 'had disclosed') is *gratia dia*: *dia* being an alternative form of *diva*, 'divine', agreeing with *gratia*, 'grace'; object is *haec armamentaria*

16. venturi … fati – genitive after *armamentaria*, future participle of *venio* = 'of a fate about to come'

17. sacri … poli – 'of holy heaven', *polus* is 'sky' or 'heaven'

18. iure – adverb, 'justifiably'

19. se iactaret – 'he would brag about himself that …'

20. tantum … gentem perdomuisse – accusative + infinitive (see Appendix), 'that he had crushed so many …'

21. procerumque – genitive of plural noun *proceres*, 'leading men' take after *tantum*

22. una – adverb, 'at the same time'; *gentem* – 'the nation'; *manu* – 'by his own hand'.

5. Samuel Johnson (1709–1784)

We have already noted that Johnson was well known for composing off-the-cuff Latin poems. Mrs Piozzi (formerly Mrs Thrale) provides one such example in her *Anecdotes of Dr Johnson*:

'One evening in the oratorio season of the year 1771 Mr Johnson went with me to Covent Garden Theatre, and though he was for the most part an exceedingly bad playhouse companion, as his person drew people's eyes upon the box, and the loudness of his voice made it difficult for me to hear anybody but himself, he sat surprisingly quiet, and I flattered myself that he was listening to the music. When we were got home, however, he repeated these verses, which he said he had made at the oratorio.'

From Mrs Piozzi's *Anecdotes of Dr Johnson*

'Molly,' says Dr Johnson, 'was a beauty and a scholar, and a wit and a Whig; and she talked all in praise of liberty: and so I made this epigram upon her. She was the loveliest creature I ever saw!!!

"*Liber ut esse velim, suasisti pulchra Maria,*
Ut maneam liber – pulchra Maria,
vale!"'

'Will it do this way in English, sir?' said I.

'Persuasions to freedom fall oddly from you;
If freedom we seek – fair Maria, adieu!'

In Theatro

Tertii verso quater orbe lustri
Quid theatrales tibi crispe pompae?
Quam decet canos male literatos
    Sera voluptas!

Tene mulceri fidibus canoris?
Tene cantorum modulis stupere?
Tene per pictas oculo elegante
    Currere formas?

Inter equales sine felle liber,
Codices veri studiosus inter
Rectius vives, sua quisque carpat
    Gaudia gratus.

Lusibus gaudet puer otiosis,
Luxus oblectat juvenem theatri,
At seni fluxo sapienter uti
    Tempore restat.

Notes:

1. Metre: Sapphics (see box)
2. tertii ... lustri – genitive; a *lustrum* is a period of five years
3. verso orbe – ablative, *verso* from *verto*, 'turn' or 'come round', so 'with the circuit of your third *lustrum* having come round four times (*quater*)'; a convoluted way of saying 60 years old!
4. theatrales ... pompae – nominative, the delights of the theatre
5. crispe – vocative; Horace addresses a Crispus in one of his *Odes* (2.2) and Johnson may be making reference to this; there was a Samuel Crisp, a friend of Johnson's club compatriot Dr Burney and the 'dear daddy' of Fanny Burney's diaries, but he lived in virtual seclusion in Chessington and in 1771 had met neither Johnson nor Thrale, nor could he be described as new to the pleasures of the theatre having years earlier tried his hand unsuccessfully as a playwright
6. decet ... male – literally 'badly suitable' so 'unseemly' or 'inappropriate'

The Sapphic Stanza

Named after the Greek poetess Sappho, this metre was used for love poetry and occasional lyric verse. It was much favoured by the great Latin poet Horace. Each stanza consists of three lines in the following pattern:

$$- \cup \mid - - \mid - \cup \cup \mid - \cup \mid - - \mid$$

The fourth line consists of just two feet:

$$- \cup \cup \mid - - \mid$$

n.b. the final syllable of each line can be either heavy or light (see Chapter 3).

7. canos … literatos – literally 'erudite white hairs', i.e. cultured or scholarly old men

8. sera voluptas – a late-coming pleasure, i.e. he is too old for theatrical delights

9. tene – a question asked by adding the enclitic –ne: 'Is it the case that …?', 'Can it be that …?'

10. te … mulceri … stupere … currere – accusative + infinitives (see Appendix)

11. fidibus canoris – ablative, literally 'resonant lyres', i.e. the musical instruments in the orchestra pit

12. modulis – ablative, the tunes or melodies

13. pictas … formas – 'painted figures', perhaps the actors and actresses in make-up, or the scenery?

14. oculo elegante – 'with a discriminating eye'

15. equales – in this stanza Crisp is exhorted to live as becomes men of his own age; sine felle – 'without bitterness' (Samuel Crisp remained ever bitter about the failure of his play, but see note 5 above)

16. codices – books, suggesting a propensity for antiquarianism

17. rectius vives – future tense of vivo; rectius – comparative adverb, 'more properly'; a quote from the opening line of Horace's Ode 2.10

18. quisque carpat – another Horatian sentiment (q.v. carpe diem), 'let each seize his own joys (sua gaudia)'

19. lusibus … restat – in the final stanza the idle games of boyhood and the diversions of the young man are contrasted with how the old man should behave

20. sed seni … restat – here restat is impersonal, 'but it remains for an old man (seni – dative)'; deponent verb utor, uti takes the ablative, hence fluxo … tempore, 'passing time'; sapienter – adverb.

6. The Author (1967–)

The art of Latin poetry never entirely died out – writing imitations of Horace has long been a pleasant diversion for Classics professors – though beyond the towers of academe it has become all but extinct. As we have seen, though, Latin poetry can be suitable for any occasion: the subject doesn't have to be lofty nor the language perfectly Ciceronian.

So here is a resolution for all you Latinists out there (yes, reader, that includes you): try to write some Latin poetry, whether you choose quantitative verse – serious hexameters, occasional hendecasyllables, lovelorn elegiacs – or accentual lyrics for celebrating and singing (musicians, why not set your words to music?). Don't be frightened by metrical theory, and don't imagine you need an encyclopaedic knowledge of the Classical poets; think instead of the pleasure you will derive from expressing your thoughts in the language of Catullus, Virgil and Horace. Read your verses aloud to yourself – relish the sound of the words – then read them to your friends and families, post them on the internet, circulate them wherever you can. Perhaps we have an opportunity to revive a venerable art.

I print the little ditty below not from motives of vanity, but simply as a demonstration that anyone can do it – even me!

Plato Mi

> Tu carissimus es caniculorum,
> Plato mi, mihi callidissimusque:
> Tu stertens quoque semper impudenter
> Stratis, me gelido, cubare raptis
> Furtive potes immemorque dormis.
> Si fortasse ruas viam iocose,
> Pellens papilionem in aere agentem,
> Tu tutus mihi, machinis vitatis,
> Reddas semper, et immemorque mortis.
> Felicissimus es caniculorum.

Notes:

1. Metre: hendecasyllables (see Chapter 3)
2. caniculorum – *canicula* (feminine) is the word for a female or little dog, but like the English word 'bitch' it is used perjoratively of people, so I have coined *caniculus* for my little (male) dog, a Cavalier King Charles Spaniel called Plato
3. Plato – Latinisation of a Greek proper name (Πλατων) – note the 'a' is short unlike the standard English pronunciation; *mi* is vocative
4. stertens – 'snoring', present participle of *sterto, stertere*
5. impudenter – adverb

6. stratis ... raptis – ablative absolute (see Appendix), 'with the sheets having been stolen'

7. me gelido – another ablative absolute, 'while I am frozen' (because the sheets have been stolen!)

8. furtive – adverb, with *stratis raptis*

9. cubare – take after *potes*, 'you can lie down'

10. immemorque dormis – 'and taking no notice you sleep'

11. si ... ruas – subjunctive of *ruo, ruere*, 'rush headlong into ...', introducing a hypothetical, 'if you should ...'

12. iocose – adverb

13. pellens – present participle of *pello, pellere*, 'driving' here in the sense of 'putting to flight'; note alliteration

14. papilionem ... agentem – *papilio* q.v. French *papillon*; *agentem* – present particple from *ago, agere*: 'fluttering on the breeze'; note elisions here: *papilion(em) in aer(e) agentem*, intended to give the line a 'flighty', rushing sound

15. tu tutus – more alliteration; take *mihi* with *reddas*, subjunctive of *reddo, reddere*: 'may you come back safe to me'

16. machinis vitatis – ablative absolute (see Appendix), *machina* here = 'car' (Italian *macchina*); *vitatis* perfect participle passive from *vito, vitare*, 'avoid'

17. immemorque mortis – *immemor* takes a noun in the genitive, here of *mors*, 'death'; note echo of line 5

18. felicissimus ... – the final line echoes the first

19. The Roman poet Martial (c.40-102) also wrote a poem about a pet dog in hendecasyllables - though the dog belonged not to him but to a friend. Like the epitaph in Chapter 3, *Quam dulcis fuit ista, quam benigna*, Martial also makes clear that his inspiration is the *passer* poems of Catullus: his begins with the line *Issa est passere nequior Catulli* (I.109). 'Issa is more mischievous than Catullus' sparrow'.

Recommended Reading:

Ashdowne, R. & Morwood, J.   *Writing Latin*
Bristol Classical Press

An easy-to-use manual on writing Classical Latin prose.

Califf, D.J.   *A Guide to Latin Meter and Verse Composition*
Anthem Classics

A rare modern book on the subject.

Money, D.K.   *The English Horace: Anthony Alsop and the Tradition of British Latin Verse*
OUP

David Money's case study of eighteenth-century Latin poet Alsop gives an overview of Neo-Latin poetry in Britain and prints Alsop's poems with English translations.

Rudd, N.   *Samuel Johnson: The Latin Poems*
Bucknell University Press

Niall Rudd's edition of Johnson's Latin poetry provides extensive notes and translations.

ENGLISH TRANSLATIONS

Caveat lector: as with the English translations in *Annus Horribilis*, you will find my renderings below distressingly literal and pedantically faithful to the originals for the purpose of elucidating the grammar. You should look upon these as the starting-point, not the end, of your own translation efforts.

Chapter I

CURSES

1. To the Divine Nodens, Silvanius has lost a ring. He has given half of its value to Nodens. Among those whose name is Senicianus do not allow good health until he shall deliver (the ring) all the way to the Temple of Nodens.

2. May (s)he who has stolen Vlbia from me become as liquid as water ... (s)he who has stolen it ... (list of names)

3. I dedicate to the goddess Minerva Sulis the thief who stole my cloak, if slave, if freedman, if man, if woman, let him not purchase this gift unless with his own blood.

4. Uricalus, his wife Docilosa, his son Docilis and Docilina, his brother Decentinus, Alogiosa – the names of those who swore an oath at the spring of the goddess Sulis on the twelfth of April. Whosoever may have sworn falsely there, see to it that he makes amends to the goddess for that with his own blood.

5. Basilia gives to the Temple of Mars a silver ring, if a slave or freedman was a witness or knows something about this let him be cursed in his blood and his eyes and all his limbs or even let him be done for with all his intestines having been eaten away, he who stole the ring or who was a witness.

COINS

1. Tiberius Claudius Caesar Augustus, High Priest, holder of the Tribunician Power, Emperor, issued by a decree of the Senate.

2. The Emperor Gordianus, faithful and fortunate, Augustus, dedicated to Eternal Rome.

THE VINDOLANDA LETTERS

1. Claudia Severa to dear Lepidina, greetings. On the eleventh of September, sister, I invite you gladly to my birthday party. Be sure that you come to us to make the day more enjoyable for me by your arrival ... I will expect you, sister. Farewell sister, my darling, so I take my leave my dearest and hail. To Sulpicia Lepidina wife of Cerialis from Severa.

2. Chrauttius sends many greetings to Veldeius his brother and old messmate and I ask you, brother Veldeius, I am surprised that you have written nothing to me for such a long time whether you have heard from our parents ... in which unit he is and you will greet him from me in my own words and Virilis the veterinary you will ask him that you send to me via one of our friends the shears which he promised to me for a price ... I pray you may be most fortunate, farewell. To Veldedeius at London, the governor's groom, from his brother Chrauttius.

Chapter 2

IAMBIC HYMNS

1. *O Quanta Qualia*

O how many and of what kind are the Sabbaths which the celestial council always celebrates. What rest for the weary, what reward for the strong, when God will be all things in everything. True Jerusalem is that city, whose peace is everlasting, the greatest delight, where desire does not anticipate fulfilment, nor is the reward for desire less. What king, what council, what palace, what peace, what rest, what that joy, let those who partake of this glory expound, if they can express how much they feel. It is ours in the meantime to raise up our hearts and seek our homeland with all our prayers, and after a long exile to return at last from Babylon to Jerusalem. In that place, after all our woes have ended, untroubled we will sing the songs of Sion, and the blessed multitude will return to you, O Lord, everlasting thanks for the gifts of grace. In that place Sabbath will follow Sabbath, the continual happiness of those celebrating the Sabbaths, nor will the unutterable cries of joy cease, which both we and the angels will chant. Let there be glory everlasting for the eternal Lord, from whom there are, through whom there are, in whom there are all things; he is the Father from whom there are, the Son through whom there are, the Spirit of the Father and the Son in which there are all things.

2. *Veni Creator Spiritus*

Come Creator, Holy Spirit, visit the souls of your own people, fill with celestial grace the hearts which you have created. You who are called the Comforter, gift of the most high God, living fount, fire, beloved, and spiritual ointment. You who are a sevenfold gift, you who are the finger of God's right hand, you who rightly according to the promise of the Father are enriching our throats with speech. Kindle a light for our senses, pour love in our hearts, fortifying the weakness of our body with perpetual virtue. May you repulse the enemy further, and may you give peace right away, with you as leader thus going ahead, may we avoid all harm. Grant that through you we may know the Father, and may we recognise the Son, and we may believe in you the Spirit of both for all time. Let God the Father have glory and the Son, who rose from the dead, and the Comforter for ever and ever.

TROCHAIC LYRICS

1. *Ave Maris Stella*

Hail, star of the sea, nurturing mother of God, and ever virgin, fortunate portal of heaven. Receiving that 'Hail' from the mouth of Gabriel, make us firm in peace, borrowing the name of Eve. Loose the bonds for the accused, bring light to the blind, drive out our evils, offer every good. Show that you are his mother, let him receive through you prayers who born for us allowed himself to be yours. Matchless virgin, gentle among all, we who have been freed from our faults make us gentle and chaste. Provide for us a pure life, prepare the safe road, so that seeing Jesus we may always rejoice. Let there be praise to God the Father, the greatest dignity to Christ, honour to the Holy Spirit, the three who are one.

2. *Huc Usque*

Until now, unhappy me, I had hidden the matter well and I loved cunningly. At last my condition was exposed, for my stomach swelled, birth follows pregnancy. Hence my mother beats me, hence my father reproaches me, both treat me harshly. Alone I sit at home, I do not dare to go out, nor to appear in public. When I do go outdoors I am gazed at by all as if I were a prodigy. When they see this womb, one nudges another, they are silent until I have passed by. Always they nudge with their elbow, they point at me with their finger, and as if I had become a marvel. With their nods they point me out, they judge that I am fit for a funeral pyre, because once I had sinned. Why should I go over every single thing? I am the talk of the town, and in the mouth of all. This grief increases, because my love is in exile on account of that trifle. I am in sorrow for his absence, in an increasing amount of grief. Because of the ferocity of his father he withdrew from the farthest borders to France. For this reason I suffer violence, now I am dying with grief, always I am in tears.

Chapter 3

HEXAMETER EPITAPHS

1. Here lies good Berta Rosata, distinguished by her good morals.

2. Here lies Arthur, king in ancient times and king who is to come.

3. (one possible interpretation only) That which was existing, that is not, that which was not existing, that is existing, because that which is not existing is existing, it will not be not existing (i.e. he who used to exist is now dead and what exists of him now [his corpse,

his memorial?] did not exist before; because his soul does exist he
who does not exist [in corporeal form] will continue to exist).

4.   They weep today at Salisbury because the sword of Justice has
     fallen, the father of the church of Salisbury, while he lived he
     nurtured the needy, nor did he fear the arrogance of the powerful,
     but was the scourge (club) and the terror of the guilty. He traced
     his ancestry from dukes and from noble princes, and he shone
     nearby like a precious jewel for you. (*or* like a precious jewel he
     shone light upon those nearby princes in turn *or* ... upon each
     of the three princes nearby.)

5.   Here lies Humphrey, formerly the distinguished Duke of
     Gloucester, protector of Henry VI, detector of an inept fraud,
     when he identified the fictitious miracle of the blind man. He
     was the light of his native country, a venerable cornerstone of
     the kingdom. A lover of peace and supporter of the nobler arts,
     whence a work that has proved popular with Oxford, the School
     of Divinity which is now resplendent. But a malevolent woman,
     worthless to the kingdom, the king and herself, destroyed him,
     scarcely having considered him worthy of this humble tomb.
     Though broken by ill-will, nevertheless he lives on after death.

ELEGIAC EPITAPHS

1.   Farewell Anna, who living long married twice, in death you are
     married a third time to God (literally: 'who was a wife to a pair
     of husbands, having died you are a wife to the triple god').

2.   The earth covers, the people mourn, Olympus holds him who
     was in discernment a Nestor, in inspiration a Socrates, in skill a
     Virgil.

3.   O little boy, I begrudge it not, you will go to the stars without
     me. O little boy, do not begrudge it, gladly will I follow you to
     the stars.

4.   The woman who lies interred beneath this marble, lived as a
     wife, a friend, a parent pure, just, pious. Alas for me that she is

in a place to which a living husband is not allowed to go. Death was life for her, while living is death for me.

5. Here you rest, O Wortley, an object of grief to your family, and yet wholly virtuous, the honour of the common people, the glory of the knights, beloved of the king. Because you were loyal to your native country, dear to the world, helpful to the needy, together they grieve that you have died. But when will religious faith, piety, constancy and virtue find a similar man? They have indeed found a similar one, but from a different sex: to such an extent is your wife similar and dissimilar to you.

HENDECASYLLABIC EPITAPH

How sweet she was, how gentle, who while she lived, lay in my lap always sharing my sleep and my bed. O it is badly done, Myia ('Midge'), that you have perished. You would just bark, if any rival, unrestrained, would lay down beside your mistress. O it is badly done, Myia, that you have perished. Now a deep grave holds you unawares, you can neither growl nor jump, nor do you grin at me with affectionate nips.

Chapter 4

1 *Cicero to Terentia*

Tullius sends greetings to his dear Terentia, his dear little Tullia and his dear Cicero. Begun at Thessalonica, finished at Dyrrachium, 58 B.C. It is reported to me both by the letters of many people and by the conversation of everyone that your steadfastness and fortitude are incredible and that you are not exhausted either by the labours of mind or body. Woe is me! That you, a woman well-known for courage, faithfulness, integrity, humanity have fallen into such troubles on my acount. And that our little Tullia, who used to take such pleasure from her father, derives grief from him. For what can I say about Cicero? Who as soon as he began to have understanding, has apprehended the bitterest sorrows and afflictions. Which if, as you write, I should consider them made by fate, I should bear them a little more easily; but everything has been brought about through my fault, I who thought that I was loved by those who were jealous of me, nor did I follow those who sought me out. See to it that you keep well and that you send couriers to me, so that I know what is being done and what you are all doing. At any rate I now have but a short time to wait. Give my regards to little Tullia and Cicero. Farewell. 25th November, at Dyrrachium.

2. Cicero to Terentia

Marcus Tullius Cicero many greetings to his dear Terentia. At Venusia, 47 B.C. I think that I will arrive at the Tusculan villa on the seventh or the day after. Let everything be made ready, for perhaps I will have many people with me and, as I imagine, I will stay for some considerable time. If there is not a basin in the bathroom, see to it that there is one. The same goes for everything else which is necessary for sustenance and good health. Farewell. 1st October, from the district of Venusia.

3. Mark Antony to Octavian

What has changed your mind? Is it because I'm shagging the Queen? Is she my wife? Have I just begun now or was it nine years ago? In that case are you shagging only Drusilla? You're doing well if, when you read this letter, you have not shagged Tertulla or Terentilla or Rufilla or Salvia Titisenia or all of them. What difference does it make, where and with whom you get a stiffy?

4. Augustus to Tiberius

We, my dear Tiberius, celebrated the festival of Minerva pleasantly enough; for we played all day long and kept the gaming-board of the gamblers warm. Your brother carried out his business amid great applause; in short however he did not lose much, but from losses great beyond hope his loss was gradually won back. I lost 20,000 coins in my own name, but after I had been lavishly generous in the game, as is generally my wont. For if I'd waived those stakes which I had called for from each player, or I had retained what I gave to each, I would have won perhaps 50,000. But I'd rather this; for my kindness shall raise me to celestial glory.

5. *Augustus to Livia*

I'll be damned if I'm not astonished that your grandson Tiberius was able to please me while declaiming. For I do not see how he who speaks so 'obscurely' is able, when he declaims, to say 'clearly' those things which need to be said.

6. *Trajan to Pliny*

Trajan to Pliny. You have followed the method which you were obliged to, my dear Secundus, in examining the cases of those who had been reported to you as Christians. For nothing can be laid down which might be regarded as a fixed arrangement. They must not be hunted down; if they are brought before you and accused, they must be punished; but in the case of anyone who has denied that he is a Christian and has made that plain in fact, that is by making offerings to our gods, however suspect he was in the past, he should obtain a pardon as a result of his repentance. Defamatory pamphlets published anonymously ought to have no place in an accusation. For it is characteristic of the worst sort of precedent nor is it of our present time.

Chapter 5

1. *Heloise to Abelard*

To her master, or rather father, to her husband or rather brother, your servant or rather daughter, his wife or rather sister: Heloise to Abelard.

The letter you sent as consolation to a friend, dearly beloved, by chance someone recently brought to me. Observing immediately from the very inscription on the front that it was yours, I began to read it so much the more eagerly as the more dearly I embrace in my heart the writer himself so that, [although] I have lost his physical presence, by his words at least I am revived as if by some likeness of him. Nearly everything I recall of this letter was filled with bile and wormwood, namely those things which related the unhappy story of our conversion and, my only love, your unremitting torments ...

God knows I never expected anything of you except yourself, desiring you unconditionally not what is yours. I did not expect treaties of matrimony, not any dowries, in short I did not devote myself to fulfilling my pleasures or desires, as you yourself know, but yours. And if the name of wife seems more holy and wholesome, the term mistress always appeared to me sweeter or, if you do not take offence, that of concubine or whore, so as no doubt the more I humbled myself for you, the more gratitude I sought in your eyes and thus also injured less the glory of your pre-eminence ...

And so by that God to whom you have offered yourself I beg you that in whatever way you can you give back to me your presence, namely by writing some consolation to me, so that by this means at least having had my strength renewed I can the more readily devote time to divine service. When formerly you sought me out for disgraceful pleasures, you visited me with frequent letters, with many a song you placed your Heloise in everyone's mouth. With my name all the streets, with my name each house resounded. But how much more properly you should now rouse me for God than then for lust? Consider, I beg, what you owe, heed what I ask, and I conclude a long letter with a brief finish: Farewell, my only love.

2. *Petrarch to Cicero*

Francis to his Cicero, greetings.

Your letters which had been long and frequently sought after and which had been found where least I imagined, I read through most eagerly. I learned about you as you were saying much, complaining of much, vacillating much, O Marcus Tullius, and long before now I had known what kind of instructor you had been to others, now at last I got to know what kind you were to yourself. Hear, wherever you are, in your turn this one thing that having arisen from true esteem is no longer a counsel but a lament, which one of your descendants, most respectful of your name, pours out not without tears.

O ever restless and anxious, or so you may recognise your own words, 'O impetuous and ill-starred old man', what did you desire for yourself by so many disputes and by feuds which would gain you absolutely nothing? When did you forsake the leisure suitable for your age and your profession and your circumstances? What sham splendour of glory entangled you, an old man, in the wars of the young and, after you had been driven hither and thither through all misfortunes, hurried you away to a death unworthy of a philosopher? Alas, unmindful of both brotherly advice and so many of your own salutary precepts, like a nocturnal traveller bearing a torch in the darkness you pointed out to those who would follow the path, on which lamentably enough you yourself went astray.

I say nothing of Dionysius, I say nothing of your brother and nephew, I say nothing, if you have no objection, even of Dolabella himself, those whom at one time you raise to the sky with praises, at another you abuse with unexpected imprecations: perhaps these things might have been endurable. I pass by Julius Caesar, too, whose admired clemency itself was a haven for those who were attacking him; moreover I remain silent about Pompey the Great, with whom by some right of familiarity you seemed to be able to do anything. But what madness drove you against Antony? Love of the Republic, I suppose, which at this very time you confessed was entirely ruined. Even if a pure faith, if liberty drew you along, why were you so familiar with Augustus? For what will be your reply to your own Brutus, 'If indeed,' he said, 'Octavian pleases you, you will seem not to have fled from a master but to have sought a friendlier one.'

This is remaining, unhappy man, and this was the last deed, Cicero, that you abused that very man whom you had so praised, who I may say was not abusing you, though he was not opposing those who were being abusive. I mourn your lot, my friend, and I am ashamed of and pity your mistakes, and now with that same Brutus 'I set no store by those arts in which I know that you were most skilled.' For to be sure what use is it to teach others, what benefit always to speak about virtues with the most splendid words, if meanwhile you would not listen to yourself? Ah, how much more preferable it had been especially for a philosopher that you had grown old in rural tranquility, 'musing on that everlasting life', as you yourself once wrote in some place, 'not about this brief span', that you had no fasces, that you had coveted no triumphs, that no Catilines had puffed up your ego. But such things indeed are in vain. Eternal farewell, my dear Cicero.

Among the living, on the right bank of the Adige, in the city of Verona, in Transpadane Italy, on the sixteenth of May, in the year from the birth of that God whom you did not know 1345.

3. *Erasmus to Dr Francis*

I am frequently accustomed both to wonder and to lament how it happens that Britain has been troubled for so many years now by an incessant plague, especially by that lethal sweat, which evil it almost seems to have uniquely. I read that a state was freed from a lengthy plague by a philosopher's plan for altering the buildings. Either my understanding deceives me or by a similar method England might be liberated.

First, they care nothing about which part of the sky the windows or doors look out on: next the rooms are generally so constructed that they are not at all ventilated, which Galen advises especially. Then they have a great part of the wall transparent with glass panes, which in this way admit light as they exclude draughts, in spite of which they admit that air filtered through small cracks, which is sometimes unhealthier after stagnating there for a long time. Sometimes the floors are covered with clay, at other times with rushes from the marshes which are now and again thus refreshed, that the floor remains sometimes for twenty years warming itself underneath spittle, vomit, spilt beer, the remains of fish and other filth not to be named. Hence a vapour is given off when the weather changes which is in my opinion the least conducive to health for the human body.

Farewell, most cultivated man, to whom I owe a great deal.

4. *Bentley to Graevius*

I grieve indeed, and now after all this time I hardly forgive myself, that I have not sooner replied to your letters, which were delivered to me more than five months ago. But you will grant, as I hope, this favour to a man both occupied by infinite tasks, and almost from that time far away from the City and absent from the company of literary men.

Lately indeed I have entirely moved back to London, where it seems that I will own a permanent home in the future, although I had no intention before than at this first opportunity to give the greatest thanks possible to you in a letter both in my name and in that of others for that most noble and divine Oration, in which you have consecrated to eternity the memory of the incomparable Queen: behold for yourself, opportunely he presents himself to me, Grodeckius who, hastening to your Batavia, will deliver this to you. And so you may know that I have taken care for your copies to be delivered, according to your instructions, to the Bishops of Salisbury, Lichfield, and Norwich, who has discussed the Philosophy of Cicero with you: but not to Doctor Smith, in other respects a virtuous and learned man; but, what you, I think, had not heard, not a little unfavourably inclined to King William and the memory of his Blessed Mary. It seemed preferable therefore, to give the copy destined for Smith to the Archbishop of Canterbury; and another, which you assigned specifically to me, to the Archbishop of York; so that you did not seem to be either ignorant or heedless of these highest Prelates no less distinguished in learning than dignity.

They all, both on account of this Oration and the infinite other tokens of your outstanding intellect, which travel to and fro through the mouths and hands of all and turn the eyes of all to you, willingly indicate that they have the greatest affection and respect for you. Farewell, most distinguished man, and love me. At London, 29th November, 1695.

5. Smollett to Dr Fizes

The patient is past his 43rd year. Constitution moist, thick, overflowing with phlegm, very often overwhelmed by catarrhs. Catarrah never not accompanied by fever, anxiety and shortness of breath. An irritation of the mucus membrane of the trachea, a cough at first dry, husky, but then bringing up a copious discharge: spittle very like the white of an egg ...

Some years ago, after youthful activities had been suddenly abandoned, he sunk into a sedentary life. With his mind directed towards more laborious studies, the fibres were gradually relaxed. During reading and writing with his body bent down, the mischief descended on his chest. A scorbutic condition assisted the violently attacking malady. The first attack was unduly scorned. He did not take measures to deal with the returning enemy. By delaying his health was not restored. His stomach recoiled from suitable remedies. With the shortness of breath worsening, in vain a phlebotomy was attempted. By the letting of blood the life-force was diminished. The pulse became weaker, breathing more difficult. Everything fell into a worse state. The irregular fever was changed into a continuous little fever. The shortness of breath was firmly established. The binding of the fibres was loosened. Good health was entirely overthrown.

While rainy winter was holding sway the pains were renewed; nevertheless in clear weather riding was a benefit to him. In the summer the malady made hardly any progress. In the autumn, with his health having declined more, he sought not in vain solace at Bath Spa. That astonishingly medicinal water, applied alike externally and internally, brings relief from evils. Another winter followed, cold, severe, long-lasting, but harmless. In the new spring a terrible calamity let loose dreadful disturbances in his mind; in his whole body, in his whole mind he was agitated. Having left his native country in sadness, worry, indignation, and the most cruel recollection pursued him. His former enemies came back with an inveterate fury. The hectic fever returned; the asthma returned accompanied by anxiety, a cough, and a tearing pain in the side.

6. *Sterne to J.H-S.*

I received your most charming letter, my cousin, dearer than all my cousins, on Friday; but the post was not going back to the North on that day, otherwise I would have written just as you desired. I don't know what is the matter with me, but I am exhausted and sick about my wife more than ever – and I am possessed with a devil who drives me to the city – and you are possessed with that same evil spirit who holds you in the wilderness to be tempted by your maidservants, and vexed by your wife – believe me, my Antony, that this is not the road to salvation whether the present or eternal; for you begin to think about money, which, as St. Paul says, is the root of all evils, and you do not say enough in your heart, I am Antony from Crazy Castle, I am now more than 40 years old, and I have completed my eighth *lustrum*, and it is time for me to look after myself, and to make that Antony of mine a happy and free man, and to do a kindness to my own self, as Solomon urges, who says that nothing is better in this life than that a man should live cheerfully and that he should eat and drink, and enjoy the good because that is his portion and dowry in this world.

Now I would wish you to know that I ought not to be censured for going in a hurry to London, because God is my witness, that I am not hastening on account of glory, and to make an exhibition of myself; for that devil who entered me, is not an empty devil, but Lucifer his cousin – but he is a devil full of love, who does not allow me to be alone; for while I am not lying with my wife, I am more 'cocky' than is proper – and I am in the way of mortals in love – and I am foolish; therefore you, my dear Antony, will pardon me, because you were in love, and you went across the sea and across the lands and you hurried just as a devil to the same place with you being driven by a devil. I have much to write to you – but I am writing this letter in a coffee-house full of noisy company, who will not permit me to think a single thought.

Greetings to my friend Panty, I will reply to his letter – greetings to my friends in the house of Guisborough, and I beg, you may believe that I am most devoted to you in the bond of cousinship and love, my dear Antony.

Chapter 6

1. *Martyr*

Such a famine oppressed his (Nicuesa's) comrades that they abstained neither from mangy dogs, which they had with them for hunting and protection, for in battles with the naked natives they made much use of dogs in this work, nor sometimes from massacred natives. For in that place neither fruit-trees nor birds, which we have said that Darien supports, were bred, and for this reason they found the land not populated by inhabitants. Some of the company agreed to buy a very thin dog, who by now was himself almost failing from hunger, they offered many pesos of gold to the owner of the dog, that is golden castellanos [coins of Castille]. They flayed the dog for eating. The mangy hide of the dog with the bones of the head still attached they threw into a nearby thicket. On the next day a certain foot-soldier chanced upon the skin which had been thrown away by his comrades now filled with worms and half-putrid, and he carried it home. Having shaken off the worms he threw the skin into a pot and cooked it, having cooked it he ate it. Many others rushed to the soup of this cooked hide with their bowls, each offering a golden castellano for each bowl of soup.

2. Copernicus

That the universe is spherical. In the first place we must point out that the universe is a globe, whether because that shape is the most perfect of all, needing no support, being a complete whole, whether because that makes the most capacious of figures, which is best suited to enclosing and preserving all things; or even because each of the most self-contained parts of the universe – I mean the Sun, the Moon and the stars – are observed in such a shape; whether because this whole seeks to be bounded, which is evident in drops of water and other liquid bodies, since they desire to be bounded by their own agency. That such a shape has been allotted to celestial bodies no one has doubted.

3. More

The island has 54 cities all extensive and magnificent, absolutely the same in language, manners, customs, the layout for all is the same, and everywhere the same appearance of things as far as the location permits. Of those which are closest to each other 24 miles separates them. None on the other hand is so solitary from which another city may not be reached on foot by the journey of a single day. Every year three citizens from each city who are senior and experienced in business gather together to consult about the communal business of the island, for Amaurot – that city because it is situated as it were in the navel of the land lies in the most convenient position for the ambassadors from all parts – is regarded as the first and foremost city. Territories have been allotted to the cities in such a satisfactory manner that from no part does any own less than 12 miles of cultivated land. From some it is actually much greater, namely in that part where the cities are separated further from each other. No city has the desire for extending its boundaries. Indeed they consider that they are more tenants of those lands which they possess, than that they are owners.

4. Camden

But where the Cherwell joins with the Isis and the most pleasant islands are scattered about by the parting of the waters, on the level plain rises the famed University of Oxford, in the Saxon tongue *Oxenford*, in the common tongue *Oxford*, our own most noble Athens, the seat of the English Muses, the pillar, the sun indeed, the eye, and the soul, and the most celebrated wellspring of letters and wisdom, whence religion, civility and learning are spread most abundantly into all regions of the kingdom. It is a splendid and stylish city, whether you admire the elegance of private buildings, or the dignity of public ones, or the healthiness and pleasantness of its situation. For wooded hills so protect the plain like a wall that, since on the one side the pestilential South wind and on the other the tempestuous West wind have been kept out, they admit only the refreshing East wind and the North wind the protector from disease, whence on account of this situation writers record that it was formerly called *Bellositum* ['charming place']. Some in the British tongue call this place *Caer Vortigern* and *Caer Vember*, and they suppose that who knows what Vortigerns and Mempricii built it. But whatever it may have been in British times, the Saxons called it *Oxford*, and evidently with the same designation as the Greeks have for their *Bosphorus* and the Germans their *Ochenfurt upon the Oder*, namely from a ford for oxen, in which sense even today *Rhid-ychen* is called by our Britains (i.e. the Welsh). Leland however by a reasonable inference derives the name from the River Ouse, which in Latin is the Isis, and reckons that it was called *Ousford*, since the river islands which the Isis here scatters about are called *Ousney*.

5. Galileo

But that which far surpassed all wonder, or which especially urged us to make all the other astronomers and philosophers aware, is this, namely that we have discovered in addition four Wandering Stars, neither known nor observed by any of those before us, which have their own orbits around a certain visible star from the number of those already known, like Venus and Mercury around the Sun, and at one time they precede it at another they follow, never deviating beyond fixed limits from it. All of which, first being illuminated by divine grace, were discovered and observed a few days ago by means of a telescope invented by me.

6. Descartes

(i)   Let me suppose therefore that not the best God, the fount of truth, but some malignant spirit, and the same being in the highest degree powerful and cunning, had applied all its industry in this matter to deceive me: I will regard the sky, the air, the land, colours, shapes, sounds and everything external to be nothing other than the triflings of dreams, by means of which he laid snares for my credulity: in the same way I will consider myself as not having hands, nor eyes, nor flesh, nor blood, nor any sense, but falsely I am imagining that I have all these things: I will remain obstinately fixed on this thought, and so, if at any rate it is not in my power to recognize anything true, but at least this is in me, that I do not assent to falsehoods, nor may that deceiver, however powerful, however cunning, impose anything on me, with my mind secure I will beware.

(ii) But I have persuaded myself that there is utterly nothing in the universe, no sky, no earth, no minds, no bodies; surely therefore that even I do not exist? On the contrary, if I persuaded myself of that I am certain I exist. But there is some unknown deceiver, in the highest degree powerful, in the highest degree cunning, who is always diligently deceiving me. If he is deceiving me, indisputably therefore I also exist; and let him deceive me as much as he can, never will he bring it about that I am nothing so long as I will think that I am something. So that, with everything having been considered more than sufficiently, finally it must be established that this proposition, I am, I exist, as often as it is uttered by me, or it is formed in my mind, is necessarily true.

Chapter 7

1. *Erasmus*

An elegy of Erasmus: full of complaints of pain. Although for me grey hairs are not yet growing on a crown becoming white with age, neither does my forehead deprived of its own hairs glisten, or a more abundant age dull the keenness of my eyes, nor does a black tooth fall from my barren mouth, and not yet do rigid hairs make my arms bristly, nor does loose skin hang from my withered body – in short I can see no proof of my having grown old – I know not what fortune and god waits upon the wretched. They desired that I bear the evils of old age during my tender years, and now they desire that I am an old man, but they do not permit me to have grown old. Already worry and pain, which shower my life with bitter old age, have arrived before their appointed day.

2. *Milton*

(i)   On the Gundpowder Plot. O treacherous Fawkes, when at the same time you ventured upon a monstrous sacrilege against the King and the British governors, am I mistaken or did you wish to seem in some degree merciful and to compensate for your crime with wicked piety? That is to say, you intended to send them to the palace of high heaven on a sulphurous chariot with flaming wheels. In such a way as he, whose head was untouchable by the fierce Fates, departed from Jordanian fields having been carried off by a whirlwind.

(ii) To Leonora while she was singing at Rome. Their own winged angel from among the heavenly ranks (believe it is so, ye nations) has been assigned to each person. What a marvel, Leonora, if you have a greater glory? For your very voice proclaims the presence of God. Either God, or at least the third mind of an empty heaven coming forth via your throat softly insinuates itself; coming forth it insinuates itself, and readily teaches that mortal hearts can become accustomed to an immortal sound. Because if there is indeed a God everywhere, and he has been given utterance through everything, in you alone he speaks, keeping the rest silent.

3. *Addison*

The little ball flies out, a marker which designates the future course; and following the track of the thrown ball, he who begins the first contest lets drop his sphere, but that having been let loose feebly traces a path which leads towards the small ball, until gradually with its first charge exhausted it stops short; suddenly one ball after another darts forth. Soon there are spread out a tight-packed throng scattered widely around the smaller little ball, and the dense mass surrounds the marker, and denies an easy approach; now more cautiously a rolling wood goes out and carefully makes its way through. But if by chance he who sent it sees that the feeble ball is creeping, and that the applied motion is suddenly growing weak, from behind he urges it on and anxiously presses on the sphere's track, and reprimands the delay, and bends over the running ball. And in order that the honour of his sluggish right hand is preserved he blames the uneven ground, and an impediment arising on the marble. Nor do they hold their laughter in check when a driven ball is rolled with a disgraceful throw, or too much lead draws its track, and its innate quality drags the sphere from the right path. Then he who threw it pours forth vain noises and with his body bent into various shapes, rebukes its errant wanderings, and gives insults to the wood. But the sphere, scorning the insults of anger, proceeds along the route it has begun, and deaf it is moved by no complaints.

4. *Gray*

(i) Oh pleasant hills of Fiesole, with your cooling breezes that do not blow too hard! Nurturing Pallas granted to them that they are the splendour of the Tuscan Apennine, and that they become hoary with her own grey-green forests. I will not see you again hereafter from the vale of the Arno encircled by colonnades, and girdled with a glistening garland of villas rising from afar on the shining ridge, nor will I marvel at the ancient temple, and the old cypresses that screen it, with its roofs above hanging roofs.

(ii) On the Fifth of November. From her sons arises a mind that scorns all those who came before, and naturally suited to attempting new paths, which knows how to inter Mars in blind hiding-places, and to keep plots hidden from the sight of the Sun; indeed, in order to deceive he does not hesitate to go into the bowels of the earth or to die himself in the same destruction. Even now he has begun the work: let that work lack a successful outcome, I hope; and let Chance forbid that which has been undertaken, I pray: nor in vain; suddenly the golden light of heaven shines out, (see!) until the dark house is revealed to the investigator; you see the fraud exposed, and the labours of death, and you marvel at the caves stinking with their own sulphur: because if the divine grace of holy heaven had not disclosed these armaments of a fate about to come, justifiably would the criminal brag about himself, that by his act of destruction he had crushed so many of the leading men and at the same time the nation with his hand.

5. Johnson

In the theatre. Since the circuit of your third *lustrum* has come round four times, what are theatrical entertainments to you, Crisp? How inappropriate is such a tardy pleasure for learned old men! Can it be that you are affected by resonant lyres? Can it be that you are dumbfounded by the tunes of the singers? Can it be that you run over the painted figures with a discriminating eye? You will live more properly free among your peers without bitterness, a student among books of truth, let each in gratitude select his own joys. The boy rejoices in idle games, the opulence of the theatre diverts the youth, but it remains for an old man to use passing time wisely.

Mrs. Thrale's translation in English Sapphics:

> When threescore years have chilled thee quite,
> Still can theatric scenes delight?
> Ill suits this place with learned wight,
>   May Bates or Coulson cry.
>
> The scholar's pride can Brent disarm?
> His heart can soft Guadagni warm?
> Or scenes with sweet delusion charm
>   The climacteric eye?

The social club, the lonely tower,
Far better suit thy midnight hour;
Let each according to his power
    In worth or wisdom shine!

And while play pleases idle boys,
And wanton mirth fond youth employs,
To fix the soul, and free from toys,
    That useful task be thine.

6. *The Author*

You are to me, my dear Plato, the dearest of little dogs, and the most cunning: stealthily having stolen the sheets you can lie down, shamelessly always snoring, too, and while I am shivering, heedless you sleep. If perhaps playfully you should rush headlong into the road putting to flight a butterfly fluttering on the breeze, may you always come back safe to me, having avoided the cars, and heedless of death. You are the luckiest of little dogs.

APPENDIX

USEFUL GRAMMAR

Some of the common grammatical constructions encountered in this book.

(1) Ablative Absolute

A noun and a participle, both in the ablative case, are often used in Latin as an independent clause (absolute meaning 'unattached', from the verb *absolvo, absolvere*, 'free, loosen'). The most common use is with the perfect participle passive ('having been x-ed'). English generally avoids this construction however, instead using words such as 'when', 'after', 'since', 'although', e.g.:

> *Confutatis maledictis*
>
> (*Annus Horribilis*, Ch. 11)
> 'With the damned having been confounded' or 'When the damned have been confounded'

> *hinc pestilenti Austro, illinc tempestuoso Zephiro excluso*
>
> (Camden, Ch. 6)
> 'since on the one side the pestilential South wind and on the other the tempestuous West wind have been kept out'

> *obfirmata mente*
>
> (Descartes, Ch. 6)
> 'with my mind (having been made) secure'

The present participle can also be used:

> *Invidia rumpente tamen post funera vixit*
>
> (Epitaph of Humphrey, Duke of Gloucester, Ch. 3)
> 'Although broken by this ill-will, nevertheless he lives on after death'

(2) Accusative + Infinitive

In Classical Latin, verbs of saying, thinking, believing, hoping, promising and so forth (*verba sentiendi ac declarandi*) are followed by the accusative + infinitive construction. This is equivalent to the 'that ...' clause in an English sentence like 'Marcus said that he was happy':

Marcus se felicem esse dixit

Which literally translates as 'Marcus said himself to be happy'. Since the infinitive (here *esse*) has no subject, we must supply the subject in the accusative – here the reflexive pronoun *se*, referring to Marcus who is the subject of the main verb *dixit*. Compare with:

Marcus Antonium felicem esse dixit
Marcus said that Antony was happy

The opposite of *dicere* in this construction is *negare*, 'say ... not' or 'deny':

qui negaverit se Christianum esse

(Trajan, Ch. 4)

'anyone who has denied that he is a Christian'

Other examples:

omnes ... se plurimum te amare et colere prolixe significarunt

(Richard Bentley, Ch. 5)

'all willingly indicate that they have the greatest affection and respect for you'

Bellositum quondam dictum fuisse produnt scriptores

(Camden, Ch. 6)

'Writers record that formerly it had been called Bellositum'

Tene mulceri fidibus canoris?

(Johnson, Ch. 7)

'Can it be that you are affected by resonant lyres?'

(3) Future Participle

The future participle is formed by adding *-urus, -ura, -urum* to the verb stem, e.g.

> *amaturus*, 'about to love', 'on the point of loving'

It can be used to express purpose:

> *Quantus tremor est futurus / quando iudex est venturus / cuncta stricte <u>discussurus</u>*
>
> > (*Annus Horribilis*, Ch. 11)
>
> 'What dread there will be when the judge will come <u>to judge</u> all things severely'

> *Scilicet hos alti <u>missurus</u> ad atria cæli*
>
> > (Milton, Ch.7)
>
> 'Doubtless you intended <u>to send</u> them to the palace of high heaven'

(4) Gerunds & Gerundives

Gerunds are <u>nouns</u>, active in meaning. Gerundives are <u>adjectives</u>, passive in meaning.

The gerund typically corresponds to '-ing' nouns in English, e.g.

> *Bethlehem adeunt, stellulam sequendo*
>
> > (*Annus Horribilis*, Ch. 12)
>
> 'They approach Bethlehem (by) following the little star'

> *consolationem uidelicet mihi aliquam rescribendo*
>
> > (Heloise, Ch. 5)
>
> 'namely by writing some consolation to me'

> *Inter legendum et scribendum*
>
> > (Smollett, Ch. 5)
>
> 'During (i.e. while he was) reading and writing'

The nominative and accusative gerund are the same as the present infinitive:

longe nitido consurgere dorso

(Gray, Ch.7)

'rising up from afar on your shining ridge'

(except when the accusative follows the preposition *ad* where the gerund ends in *–ndum*)

The <u>gerundive</u> is an adjective, passive in meaning: 'to be -ed':

aliasque sordes non nominandas

(Erasmus, Ch. 5)

'other filth not to be named'

pellem in ollam coquendam coniecit

(Martyr, Ch. 6)

'he threw the hide into the pot to-be-cooked'

When the gerundive is accompanied by *esse* it implies obligation: translate in English as 'ought', 'must', 'have to', e.g.

conquirendi non sunt

(Trajan, Ch. 4)

'They must not be hunted down'

Principio advertendum nobis est

(Copernicus, Ch. 6)

'in the first place we must point out (that ...)'

Following certain verbs of entrusting and undertaking (*curo, suscipio* etc.) and in agreement with a noun it indicates something is caused to be done, e.g.

admonitos faciendos ... nos impulit

(Galileo, Ch. 6)

'(it) urged us to make (them) aware'

(5) *ut* + subjunctive

This construction expresses either:

a result (negative *non*), 'so .... that (not)':

> *te obsecro, ut ... tuam mihi praesentiam reddas*
>
> (Heloise to Abelard, Ch. 5)
>
> 'I beg you that you give back your presence to me'

> *enim ita obvallant nemorosi colles ut ... tantum serenantem Eurum et Aquilonem ... admittant*
>
> (Camden, Ch. 6)
>
> 'for the wooded hills so protect (the plain) that they only admit the East and North winds'

or purpose (negative *ne*), 'in order to ... (not)':

> *ne falsis assentiar*
>
> (Descartes, Ch. 6)
>
> '(in order) not to assent to falsehoods'

The negative *ne* + present subjunctive is sometimes used instead of the imperative:

> *ne nos inducas in tentationem*
>
> (*Annus Horribilis*, Ch. 9)
>
> 'do not lead us into temptation'

INDEX

Also available from The History Press

ANNUS HORRIBILIS

LATIN FOR EVERYDAY LIFE

www.thehistorypress.co.uk

Look out for the third in this series:

BRITANNICA LATINA

2000 YEARS OF BRITISH LATIN

forthcoming in 2009